Books by David Hapgood

Africa: From Independence to Tomorrow

Africa (in the series "Today's World in Focus")

With Max F. Millikan:

No Easy Harvest: The Dilemma of Agriculture
in Underdeveloped Countries

agents of change

A CLOSE LOOK AT THE PEACE CORPS

agents of
change

A CLOSE LOOK AT THE PEACE CORPS

by David Hapgood

• Meridan Bennett

LITTLE, BROWN and COMPANY

Boston   Toronto

Published simultaneously in Canada
by Little, Brown & Company (Canada) Limited

PRINTED IN THE UNITED STATES OF AMERICA

to H. C. N.

**Without whom this book would
never have been written**

acknowledgments

This book is anything but official. The Peace Corps has generously given us permission to draw on reports that we and others have written for the agency. But no one has tried to influence, still less censor, what we have to say. The authors, therefore, bear full responsibility for the contents.

Between us, we have evaluated seventeen overseas programs and visited many more, our travels covering three continents. Charles Peters, who headed the Peace Corps Division of Evaluation from 1962 to the spring of 1968, has helped us in ways too numerous to mention. The unique process of self-criticism known in the Peace Corps as evaluation would never have existed without Charlie Peters' courage and imagination. No one loves a critic; but Peters always supported us when the going got rough. We also thank the various people, in and out of the Peace Corps, who gave us permission to quote them, and Mrs. Donna Welensky, who made the text legible.

David Hapgood would like to extend particular thanks to the Center for International Studies of New York University, under whose auspices his work was completed.

Identifying people and places could at times prove embarrassing to both. When a volunteer is identified by a first name only, that name is fictitious; when full names are given, they are real.

Volunteers are what the Peace Corps is all about, and they are what this book is all about. Hundreds of volunteers in out-of-the-way corners of this world have not only taken time to answer the questions of two nosy visitors; they also gave us shelter, shared with us their food and drink, and permitted us to know their friends—allowed us to share with them some part of their encounter with the third world. Their experience, as they permitted us to see it—*insisted*, in many cases, for volunteers typically are immensely concerned with conveying the reality of their situation — is the human fabric of which this book was made. The book, therefore, has many anonymous collaborators.

D. H. and M. B.

agents of change

A CLOSE LOOK AT THE PEACE CORPS

chapter 1

A NEW EXPRESSION OF
AN OLD IDEA

The Peace Corps, in the seventh year of its existence, has become an accepted part of the federal establishment. By the standards of domestic politics, this new agency for overseas service, created in 1961 by the late President Kennedy, has been a success. The American public views the Peace Corps with approval, if not necessarily with understanding. No extravagant scandals have marred its record. Congress looks on the Peace Corps with favor. Congressmen who belabor United States foreign policy almost always exempt the Peace Corps, and the agency's budget has sailed through virtually unscathed while other foreign appropriations were being slashed.

Domestic approval alone does not, of course, tell us much about the Peace Corps record overseas. Our purpose, in examining that record in the chapters that follow, is to describe the lessons of the Peace Corps experience as we see them. That experience has taught mány Americans a great deal about the world of poverty, politely called "less developed" — the nations in which Peace Corps volunteers serve. The Peace Corps experience has also taught us lessons, not all of them pleasant, about the American culture from which the volunteers are drawn. In learning about other societies, people involved in the Peace Corps, including ourselves, have come to see their own society in a different light.

The Peace Corps cannot be understood in isolation from the America that produced it. The Peace Corps is no exotic flower. It is as everyday American as a community chivaree or Judge Roy Bean's frontier law. It came into being as a bureau of the U.S. Government, but it was backed by the public relations of Madison Avenue's image makers, and, at the same time, by the quiet concern of individual, thoughtful Americans who were not content to choose a life of easy affluence as their college graduation present. The Peace Corps conflicts of purpose, and its ambiguities in execution, are extensions of those same puzzling currents in domestic life. We may ask of any nation what it is doing, where it wants to go. In the case of the United States the lack of answers is no more pronounced than in Ghana or Costa Rica, but infinitely more dangerous, given the destructive power that lies in the American hand. The Peace Corps has helped to provide some answers — has shed light and perhaps even some heat — on the question of what American desires abroad mean.

While those answers are often ambiguous, the story of a volunteer overseas is always clear and immediate.

He is operating in a culture different from his own — often radically different and exotic. Other cultures are complex, just as the American is. They are full of quirks which a volunteer can mistake for malign strokes of fate. Few strokes have fallen more swiftly than the one which fell on Marjorie Michelmore, a volunteer in the first group to go to Nigeria in 1961. Miss Michelmore, exercising a prerogative built into her own culture, wrote a postcard home undramatically and factually describing her new surroundings. In her own culture, to read another person's mail just isn't done; in Nigeria, regardless of propriety, it was done. Miss Michelmore became the first Peace Corps *cause célèbre*, expelled by the angry Nigerians whose view of criticism Miss Michelmore, too late, came to know.

The Peace Corps of Miss Michelmore and other volunteers is not the Peace Corps created in the agency's public affairs office in Washington; nor is it the still less realistic one created in the minds of millions of Americans who want to believe that their country is capable of doing *something* good overseas and have therefore invested the Peace Corps with a degree of magic, self-sacrifice and piety which seldom, if ever, are to be matched in the field. The Peace Corps experience is a story of Americans, most of them young, finding themselves abroad, and of an American govermental agency finding answers to development problems in the hungry nations, losing them, and finding them again. It became a reality on the American scene after the presidential campaign of 1960, when questions of national purpose brought forward a promise by John F. Kennedy to form a voluntary overseas service as an arm of the U.S. Government.

When this organization was created by executive order in March, 1961, few of the those involved in its birth knew where it was to take them in the ensuing years— or even cared much, for the promise of youth and idealism seemed to them such a novel quality in government that it couldn't help but bring something important to pass. By the fall of 1961, after the first summer's frantic activity, something had, indeed, come to pass. Four hundred volunteers were already in the field, in Colombia, Chile, Ghana, Nigeria, Pakistan, the Philippines, Tanganyika and the West Indies.

The early programs were to crystallize much that is present today in the Peace Corps. That first summer's frenetic push to get a new government agency in business was repeated with increasing tempo all through the next year. It was a year in which some politicians said things about youth, callow idealism and the federal government ("Kennedy's Kiddie Korps" was one wisecrack) which they later came to regret. It was a year in which the innate conservatism of the old-line overseas agencies of the U.S. Government, notably the State Department and AID (Agency for International Development) came to the fore. It was they who grumbled loudest about the "new barbarians" and, in resisting the new agency, resembled the stereotypes in a bad novel which was also an influential polemic, Lederer and Burdick's *The Ugly American*.

The main novelty about the Peace Corps was its official sponsorship by the government. The tradition of volunteerism runs deep in American society, and for generations Americans had been traveling to the dark places of the earth to shed their light and explore. Other industrialized nations had been involved in voluntary youth movements, including some without religious affiliation or overt missionary purpose, for many years prior to the Kennedy administration's adaptation of the idea. These, however, had been private in sponsorship and funds, with no more than the tacit approval of governments. It was left to the United States to make the idea into official policy and to back that policy with the power of the national treasury. Such a sponsorship would not necessarily free the movement (for this is what the Peace Corps rapidly showed signs of becoming) from the traditional mentality of church missions. It was in the missionary context that many Americans had first tasted the enlightenment and frustrations of living in strange cultures, and their experience was part of the Peace Corps inheritance. Yet there was something more secular in the unwritten ideology of the Peace Corps — a determination to live a part of the American Dream that had not yet found expression in action. Americans wanted to be loved, and, in doing so, to find ways to help those to whom affluence is an unknown state of being. The decade of the fifties had produced a vast array of failures of American assistance abroad; whether this failure was the cause, or whether gratitude is simply a hard emotion to live with, the nations being helped were becoming increasingly churlish toward their supposed benefactor in the sixties.

The Americans who were attracted to the Peace Corps in its first year were, in many respects, a remarkable group. Their like has not been seen since. They were people of various ages and conditions who felt impelled to make some personal contribution in those poor na-

tions which the French call the third world. Their
motivation was significantly higher than that of many
of the volunteers in succeeding years: it must have been,
for although the psychic hardships of those first programs were greater than anything experienced since,
only a handful of the early volunteers came home before their two years were up. They were the trailblazers.
Many returned after two years to take up positions on
the Peace Corps staff, ceded by a nervous and insecure
bureaucracy which had not had intimate experience
with life in the third world. Many of the early pioneers
in the Peace Corps had skills relevant to the jobs they
were placed in overseas: public works, teaching, health,
and rural action. They were older than subsequent
groups, although still relatively youthful. The large
majority of them had college degrees and were representative of upward-moving, middle-class America.

The volunteers were sent overseas under a set of
institutional goals provided by Congress in the Peace
Corps Act (PL 87-293) of September 22, 1961. Three
broad objectives were stipulated by Congress. In para-
phrase, these were: (1) to help the countries inviting
volunteers to meet their needs for trained manpower;
(2) to promote abroad a better understanding of Americans and American society; and (3) to promote in the
American people a broader understanding of other
peoples. So broad were these objectives that they were
at once impossible to achieve and at the same time per-
missive of a whole range of wild experiments. Some who
came to Washington in the first years of the Peace Corps
only found out about the objectives under which they
were supposed to be working months after having gone
overseas to set up the first programs.

A turning point in Peace Corps history came early in its second year, 1962, when it was decided by the agency's director, Sargent Shriver, President Kennedy's brother-in-law, to go for broke in expanding his agency. The political gamble involved in so seemingly harebrained a scheme as the Peace Corps had paid off. The critics were giving way. The public reaction was spontaneously positive. In this year the Peace Corps decided, not just to double, but to go for a fivefold increase in membership in the span of a couple of months, from one thousand to five thousand. The fact that the goal was not reached in 1962 should not obscure what actually happened. Four thousand volunteers were overseas by the end of the year. It was a gigantic accomplishment, one which nearly killed the agency through confusion and barrel-scraping for warm bodies; but it worked. Since then the Peace Corps has grown steadily, always falling short of its own wildly optimistic growth projections, but always achieving an increase of sizable proportions. The fabulous Sargent Shriver, able to attract a steady stream of new blood into the agency, pushed restlessly for new ideas, new areas of growth and new approaches to bureaucracy. He himself was youthful and attractive, athletic and superbly in command of himself before the public and congressional committees. It was a time in which the Beautiful People had taken over. They could do anything, including make their own myths. Vietnam was only a rumble on the horizon. Watts had not yet happened. The Peace Corps appeared to be fulfilling its early promise by doing incredible things while, admittedly, making its share of mistakes. ("How could you go by the book when the book hadn't been written yet?" said officials of the agency.) It had established itself, under President Kennedy's protection, as a semi-independent arm of the overseas establishment. Americans of all ages, but particularly young college graduates, were volunteering in ever-larger numbers. Size, that inevitable measuring stick of progress in America, was rapidly making the Peace Corps an entity to be reckoned with in Washington. Peace Corps employees began to be appointed to ambassadorial posts. A Lyndon Johnson protégé, Bill Moyers, not yet turned thirty, was appointed Shriver's deputy.

Then came the assassination of John Kennedy. While the nation and the world mourned, the Peace Corps went through its own particularly intense grief at the loss of its leader. Having been a member of the agency at that moment of history clearly marked a watershed between Peace Corps generations. Nearly seven thousand volunteers in service overseas witnessed at first hand the unprecedented and perplexing phenomenon of John Kennedy's universal popularity as a figure of hope among the world's defeated and destitute.

The Peace Corps survived the loss of Kennedy and went on with the support of Lyndon Johnson. Bill Moyers moved to the White House, quickly became one of Johnson's closest advisers and, at the same time, the chief friend of the Peace Corps at court. Young men with their eye on a government career began to choose the Peace Corps route. In 1965 the agency staged its first (and to date last) giant rally of returned volunteers, convened portentously in the marble halls of the Department of State. New countries were added to the original Peace Corps hosts; the total reached fifty-six in 1967. Men of vision like Harris Wofford began to talk of new roles for the Peace Corps — a university in dispersion, an anti-establishment organization funded by the establishment. Shriver agreed to take on the building of an organization to spearhead the War on Poverty, in addition to his Peace Corps tasks. Warren Wiggins, who succeeded Moyers as Shriver's deputy, talked of a Peace Corps with a membership of towering proportions; and though the great "quantum jump" in numbers never occurred, the organization continued to grow until, at the beginning of 1968, it had twelve thousand volunteers overseas, with another seventeen hundred in training.

Shriver, himself a newcomer to Washington, built the Peace Corps as President Kennedy built much of his administration — by drawing into public life men and women who had not previously aimed their sights at careers in government. They came streaming into Washington largely ignorant of what was impossible in government operations. They had a sublime disdain for the red tape of accounting records and approved fiscal policies. To supplement the work of the amateurs, Shriver obtained a core of old pros from other federal agencies — mainly the State Department and AID. To these veterans often fell the task of sorting out the amateurs' tangled can of worms. Yet there was not an inordinate amount of conflict between the pros and the talented amateurs. Many of the latter proved themselves extraordinarily capable of surviving the rapid shifts of power in the agency, and astounded the old pros with their ability to learn the skills of bureaucratic infighting.

Shriver remained committed to bringing new faces into the agency. He even managed to get Congress to

write a five-year limitation on staff appointments to the
Peace Corps, thereby insuring that no professional personnel system would evolve. "In, up and out" was the
cry; many of the old pros went back to the State Department and AID. Amateurs also drifted away into private organizations or were snatched up by other government agencies eager for young blood. There was a tremendous loss involved in the rotation system: each time
someone left he took with him several years of priceless
experience in living and working abroad in this new venture. But Shriver was willing to pay that price to keep
the organization young and innovative — to prevent
the Peace Corps from settling into bureaucratic routine.

From the moment of its creation the Peace Corps
was one of the finest flowers of the post-Roosevelt liberal
era: intelligent, rational in its refusal to be bamboozled
by arbitrary rules, highly literate, and dependent upon
verbal expression. It contained some of the intellectual's
hubris which other observers have described as a characteristic of the New Frontiersmen. Civil informality
was also around in quantity: first names without undue familiarity was the tone. Church membership and
athletic prowess were valued, if only as secondary virtues;
there were practically no dingy, bible-clutching funda-
mentalists around, and very few people who didn't look
fairly bursting with good health. The direct opposites
of this stereotype were also cultivated in token proportion as well: a few cadaverous types with hollow coughs,
a few bold atheists and freethinkers, a couple of bearded
iconoclasts (Shriver's personal aversion to beards was an
early caveat to all postulants), some sandaled and lip-
stickless girls.

Though it depended entirely upon the performance of the volunteers in the field for its reputation and success, the Peace Corps nonetheless from the start created two separate organizations: one a paid, professional staff, and the other comprising volunteers. At all times, everywhere, volunteers have responded to the question, "Do you feel a sense of identity with the Peace Corps as an organization?" with a quiet but nearly unanimous, "No." Held at arm's length by that official "Peace Corps," they cared little about identifying themselves with it. However, they cared intensely about the idea and the fumbling attempts at its execution overseas. Gradually the volunteers welded themselves together into their own unspoken fraternity, a class apart from the Washington staffer who often did not command a second language and stiffened noticeably before a bowl of foreign food.

The creation of a separate category for volunteers separated headquarters from field operations as effectively as the State Department's traditional structure. But it also contained the seeds of its own revision. Volunteers began coming back from the field to Washington jobs, anti-authoritarian to a considerable degree. They began to weave their way into the agency's hierarchy, then up the ladder of power. Quickly they formed an amorphous underground, and even though the Peace Corps did its unconscious best to hire only those returned volunteers who looked to be most docile, the new wave began to be felt in the higher councils of power. They have been an important force for change.

Meanwhile, a war of ever-greater proportions continued to grow in Southeast Asia. The Dominican Republic, in 1965, furnished evidence within our own hemisphere of how far the United States was willing to go to counter Communist influence close to home. The nation seemed to have reached the stage of development where a burgeoning war and an expanding domestic economy could coexist. At the same time as national priorities were shifting toward military activities, the decay of American cities was becoming more apparent, as well as other domestic ills such as environmental pollution. Opportunities for idealistic youth to invest their commitment and energy multiplied, with various social programs such as VISTA (based on the Peace Corps); but the clarity of national purpose that characterized the early Kennedy years was fading in the heat of new, more troubled politics.

Americans continued to apply for the Peace Corps, though the end of 1967 saw the beginning of a decline from the 1965–1966 high of forty thousand applications per year. (The extent of that decline was uncertain, ranging from 15 percent to 35 percent, depending on whose figures you took; it was, however, a source of growing alarm to the expansion-minded agency.) About half the applicants were invited to attend Peace Corps training, and half of those invited actually accepted and showed up at the training site. Three-quarters of these made it through training and went overseas.

The profile of the Peace Corps volunteer has become clearer as the number of volunteers has increased. The great majority are between twenty and twenty-five years old, and just short of two-thirds are male. Most are single, though married couples are accepted. The "typical" volunteer, the infantryman of the Peace Corps, is what the agency calls the "B.A. generalist": a college graduate who majored in the liberal arts and went into the Peace Corps upon graduation. Although no degree is required to join the Peace Corps and there is no upper limit on age, non-college and older volunteers have been relatively few in number. Few, also, are professional people and working-class applicants. Blue-collar types are not, generally speaking, at home in the Peace Corps, whose style is that of the educated and verbal middle-class liberal. Applicants are divided into "prime" and "non-prime" categories according to whether they will hold a college degree when they enter the Peace Corps. Thus a college senior with no work experience is "prime," while a skilled non-college farmer is not. Despite the agency's preference for those who hold the symbol of a degree, people from all walks of life have volunteered, been accepted and proved themselves overseas.

All sections of the United States are represented in the Peace Corps, but the West Coast has always led in the number of volunteers per capita — perhaps because the westering urge of Americans, having come up against the wet finality of the Pacific Ocean, is seeking new directions.

The college senior who goes straight into the Peace Corps is not entirely typical of his college group. When he is compared with the rest of his class, we find that he is more likely to come from a family of college graduates. Perhaps this is because the child of a non-college family is under parental pressure to get started on a "serious" career; the college family, more secure in income and social status, can more easily accept the idea of a two-year delay in earning a living. This means that volunteers tend to come from the established groups in our society, notably the WASPs (White-Anglo-Saxon-Protestants). Minority groups are underrepresented in the Peace Corps. For example, the proportion of Negroes in the Peace Corps is far less than the percentage of Negroes in the general population, despite repeated recruiting efforts, although the agency has an outstanding record of non-discrimination.

The "B.A. generalist," of which the Peace Corps is largely composed, brings the agency little in the way of technical skills. He is, by contrast, strong in the verbal skills taught by the colleges. His motives in joining are as varied as the number of volunteers. They may range from a missionary urge to convert the heathen, to a desire to get away from home to, among males, a reluctance to face the Selective Service system. Many are attracted by the challenge of living under hard conditions — this is known as the "mud-hut image" in the Peace Corps. Most volunteers we have known, however, are motivated by an idea that was best expressed by Peggy Anderson, who served for two years as a teacher in the tiny African nation of Togo:

Most people who join the Peace Corps have no idea what it will really be like, but we who become volunteers do have some general notions. One is involvement — we expect to learn about another culture from its root hairs on up; and we hope, through that knowledge, to gain intimacy with the new environment. Another is help — we expect to be useful to the host country by doing work that needs doing. A third is survival, both

physical and spiritual — we expect, you should forgive
the term, hardship, or challenges of various kinds, that
will test and temper us as individuals. I believe that these
elements — in proportions that vary from person to person — constitute the basis of what most applicants understand as the "volunteer experience."

Along with the volunteers, the Peace Corps overseas
staffs are vital to its success or failure. Usually there is
one overseas staff person for about forty volunteers,
though the ratio differs greatly from country to country
and year to year in one country. Many Americans are
surprised to hear there is an overseas staff. Apparently it
is part of the Peace Corps mystique that the volunteers
need no supervision or support in their efforts. Yet the
leadership of the country representative (or "rep," as he
is usually called) and the support of his field officers
can make the difference between a program in which volunteers wallow in misery or idleness for two years and
one in which they turn their hands to useful and satis-
fying work.

Washington is the home of headquarters personnel,
who get the money from Congress, recruit applicants
on college campuses and in special areas such as agriculture, recreation, education and labor unions. Washington also arranges for the training of volunteers, generally
through contracts with colleges and universities across
the country. Washington is the home of various other
offices which try to keep on top of the progress of the
overseas programs and conduct the housekeeping
chores of an agency with a budget of more than $100
million. And, of course, Washington is the location of

the Peace Corps director. The present director, Jack
Vaughn, replaced Shriver early in 1966, when the latter
took over leadership of the Office of Economic Opportunity as a full-time job. Vaughn first came to the Peace
Corps from the Foreign Service in 1961 as regional
director for Latin America. He subsequently was appointed Ambassador to Panama, then became Assistant
Secretary of State for Latin America and the Alliance
for Progress, from which post he returned to the Peace
Corps as director.

Despite the generally favorable impression the Peace
Corps has made on the American public, not many
people have any clear idea of what in fact the agency
and its volunteers have been doing. "How [or *what*]
is the Peace Corps doing?" is a question Peace Corps in-
siders are asked over and over.

The question is more easily asked than answered.
The Peace Corps consists of thirty thousand individual
experiences — the number of volunteers sent overseas
as of the beginning of 1968. Each of those experiences
has its own meaning, some clear, some ambiguous. No
one, including ourselves, is familiar with more than a
minority of those cases. Beyond that, however, is the
deeper problem that no one is sure what constitutes
"success" for a volunteer overseas. Many of the effects
(if any) of his presence will not make themselves felt till
years after he has left. For some, sheer survival for two
years is some kind of accomplishment. Other volunteers
can look back and say: "I did the job I was asked to
do." But even this does not necessarily spell success,
for, as we shall see in later chapters, many volunteers
have come to question the relevance of the work they
were sent to do. In the long run, that questioning may

be more important than the original job to which they were assigned, for, as of now, what the Peace Corps has learned is certainly more important than what it has accomplished.

Surprisingly little has been written about the Peace Corps that would help answer the public's questions. While a good deal of picture-postcard propaganda and ephemeral nonsense has been published about the agency, only recently have books of greater merit begun to appear. One is a work of research on selection of volunteers for community development programs, *Volunteers for Peace* by Morris Stein, a ground-breaking attempt to say something about what it takes to succeed in the difficult job of community development. Another work is *Cultural Frontiers of the Peace Corps*, a thick M.I.T. compendium edited by Robert B. Textor. Bearing contributions by people identified as social scientists not on the Peace Corps payroll, this book tackles the Peace Corps experience as a meeting of differing cultures. The individual contributions take up in some detail Peace Corps operations in fourteen countries and are a gold mine of information, not only about the Peace Corps, but about the countries themselves. The serious student can find in this book a description of almost all of the problems that have beset the young agency, along with perceptively stated examples. But the book misses a few important difficulties of the Peace Corps that touch on the realm of practical politics in the United States. Several volunteers have also published accounts of their experiences. Of these, the most impressive is *An African Season* by Leonard Levitt, who taught in Tanzania.

Little serious attention has been paid to the effects

of the Peace Corps at home. In later chapters we take up the impact of the Peace Corps on American higher education and the long-term effect of the volunteers on their society after they come back. In the last two years there has been a certain amount of fuss in the press about the problems of returning volunteers. However, in our experience, the number of disoriented ex-Peace Corpsmen wandering the streets in search of a role has been vastly exaggerated and may, indeed, be one of those non-problems with which the mass media period- ically confront us. David Riesman has said, "The return- ing Peace Corps volunteer belongs, as yet, to a relatively small elite. He has had a chance for an unusual form of service abroad, and, as a result, he will often find upon returning that he can scarcely communicate with his old friends, whose lives have not been touched in the same way." What Riesman is talking about is an in- grained part of the American experience, what Thomas Wolfe wrote about, what traditionally happens to young Americans when they blossom outside their own back- yards. Such Americans remain aliens in their societies until they find ways of working themselves back into the fabric of their own culture — until they manage to go home again. All we can be sure of now is that the United States needs people who have successfully lived and worked in cultures radically different from their own to explain that wide differences in the way people do things do not necessarily spell defeat for the dream of human progress.

Today the Peace Corps is an accepted option for the young of the United States. It is what Morris Stein has called a "psychosocial moratorium," a time to prepare for full adulthood. The role of the Peace Corps at home that has been best fulfilled has been to provide a vehicle for expressing the helping urge outside the narrow confines of religious missions overseas. Thus it has made of itself a training ground for agents of change. At the same time, the Peace Corps has been filling another role. It has been a kind of pilot project for a new face on American foreign policy. In this role it has not fared so well. With the United States Government represented overseas by the State Department, the military and the CIA, as well as the Peace Corps, it is inevitable that the face America turns to the world will be a composite. While the Peace Corps, the smallest of these, has done well with its own image abroad, it is hardly probable that it has much changed what foreigners think of the American government. It is even less likely that it has influenced the other government agencies to change the way they represent the United States abroad.

Though the Peace Corps may decline, lose its fresh appeal, or be forced to cut back its overseas programs, there is little likelihood that it will soon vanish from the scene. Today it retains a strength acquired during its first days: it is able to avoid freezing in a mold by learning about its mistakes through remarkably — often brutally — honest feedback from the field. Its main weakness, likewise, remains with it today: it is often unable to overcome its own cultural problems, residing beneath the thinking of officials and volunteers. Perhaps the explanation is that these problems are the problems of American civilization. It is this thought that prompts a more detailed search for meaning in the Peace Corps

experience. Marjorie Michelmore's affray with the Nigerians was merely one of thousands of Peace Corps
tales written upon the water. The meaning of the experience is much harder to come by than the description
of it. This feeling of elusiveness is something volunteers
share with soldiers returning from war. The personal
meaning of a deep and shocking confrontation is, we suspect, something not quickly intellectualized or understood.

chapter 2

INTERVENING IN THE AFFAIRS OF OTHERS

Visionaries, saints and ascetics, Thoreau led us to hope, cock their ears for the beat of a different drummer. The revolutionary leaders of today certainly follow a different cadence, believing as they do that the huge army of the downtrodden will set the pace for our times.

American civilization, bewitched by its own rhythm, the Big Beat of affluence, is most concerned to protect what it has and will most probably not support the drastic steps needed to create an equal environment of plenty in the third world — this, at any rate, is the gloomy conclusion of economist Robert Heilbroner (in the April 1967 *Commentary*). Whether one concurs with Heilbroner or not, it is a fact that from the midpoint of the twentieth century onward the United States has been intervening in the affairs of other nations with ever-increasing energy. The Peace Corps is part of that movement. It has involved itself in other countries deliberately to effect some kind of change. What kind of change, and where it should be applied, has been one of the most argued-over and elusive aspects of the agency.

In point of fact, the Peace Corps Act makes no mention of directed change. But few, if any, Peace Corps volunteers follow the doctrine that they are working overseas merely to observe new, exotic ways of life, and that their jobs are not intended in some way to work changes in the countries that are their hosts. Certainly no program proposal submitted by field offices around the world to Washington headquarters takes that line. The idea of doing something positive and concrete to effect change and to solve problems in the third world is an implicit assumption of almost everything the Peace Corps has done.

An example: there is a Latin American site containing three volunteers who have labored long and hard to bring a cooperative into existence. The cooperative's members are highland Indians, historically suppressed and exploited by the local mestizos (people of mixed ancestry). The country program under which the three volunteers work originated when the host country and the United States Government signed an instrument, called in diplomatic terms a bilateral agreement, indicating mutual desire to establish a group of American volunteers in the country for the purposes described under the Peace Corps Act. The agreement specified that the volunteers were coming to the host country at its invitation and were to work under programs of the inviting government, with no protections and immunities other than those provided any citizen of that country. On the face of it, the agreement bore no note of compulsion on the part of the United States nor submission on the part of the host country. In this sense the presence of the Peace Corps in that country could not be called "intervention" under international law.

Yet what the volunteers were doing in their remote village must certainly be called interference in the affairs of that forgotten, static community. One of them was articulate on the point: "We're not just here for the good of our souls. We're here to change things. Ninety percent of the people here have no political voice. The few mestizos around are not prevented from gouging them in any way they want. The co-op helps the Indians do something about it."

Despite the punctilious appearance of nonintervention in the official documents, *de facto* intervention is a fair description of the Peace Corps work at almost any volunteer site around the world. Among the officials in Washington who plan the agency's overseas work, the talk is all about the Peace Corps as a more effective agency of directed change. Arguments rage over whether to favor measurable impact over "intangible" or longer-term benefits to the host countries, but never over whether the Peace Corps should be involved in promoting change in the first place.

The kind of change the Peace Corps might achieve is not easily measured. When AID invests dollars in a project, the economic return on the investment can be calculated. But the Peace Corps creates an intensely personal encounter between volunteers and the people of

the third world, and therefore it is working in the much
less tangible field of human development. If we are
to understand both the peril and the promise of Peace
Corps intervention, we must first of all have some understanding of the human environment into which the
volunteers are sent.

Despite the endless variety of the third world, ranging from a peaceful African village to the seething slums
of Calcutta, poverty imposes some general realities
upon the human condition.

The characteristics of the human beings who live in
isolation from the means to realize their potential are
recognizable anywhere in the world as the heart of the
syndrome of poverty: dependency, suspicion, hostility,
personal inadequacy. The victim of the syndrome often
sees his very survival as beyond his control. The good
things in his world appear to him to be strictly limited.*
This is his economics: the pie is fixed in size; all one can
do is to redivide it. He is not motivated to achieve, because by achieving he cuts someone else out of the good,
and his society has developed stringent penalties against
meddling with the general welfare. As a result, he is
suspicious of the people he has grown up with, unwilling to extend them confidence enough to cooperate in
mutually beneficial projects, often even too suspicious
to place confidence in members of his own family, the
last refuge of the isolated man. He meets the outside world with hostility, and frequently the familiar
world as well. In dealing with the problems of making a
living, of providing shelter and food, of learning to be
responsible enough to keep that job, he displays a per-

* Anthropologist George M. Foster calls this viewpoint the "image
of limited good."

sonal inadequacy which he often articulates in defense of his dependency. Hope is a luxury he cannot afford.

The men who control the institutions under which he lives often exploit him; or, if they actually seek to improve his lot, are incapable of dealing with the complexities of his situation. Malnutrition and disease weaken his ability to perform effectively in a world that increasingly demands effectiveness. These characteristics of poverty prevent the ordinary man of the poor nations from dealing with forces outside himself, which, in the twentieth century, bear in upon him with ever-accelerating speed, worsening his situation and building higher barriers from year to year against his chances for solving his problems.

Whatever security he may have — a certain amount of solidarity in the community immediately surrounding him, the feeling of predictability that a static culture provides, a system of paternalism that denies him choice in his affairs yet shields him from anxiety by removing the need to choose — is being eroded by his inability to deal with forces bearing from the outside. These forces are numerous and often subtle: the ability to read (his father could not), intimations of new and disturbing ideas, the availability of manufactured goods (his father used only what he could make or barter), the existence of roads, the cinema with its fantastic view of pseudo-life, the transistor radio. In most communities where the Peace Corps works, these forces are a fact, and their compound effect is to make the resident of those communities suffer the increasing disintegration of his social fabric.

Change is a threat. The citizen of the underdeveloped

world tends to be inflexible, to resist that which is new. If, in fact, the character patterns of people in developing countries had already evolved sufficiently to make change a positive value (as in our culture, where New! Just Out! The Latest Thing! sells everything from religion to razor blades) there would be little need for a Peace Corps. New technology would be easily absorbed — cows would be vaccinated, fertilizer applied, water boiled, medicare a blooming fact, and zip-top pop waiting in the gloaming.

Change in this century comes unbidden, a disturbing intruder in the midst of traditional, static people whose personalities, formed by tradition, cause them to resist change until poverty becomes a culture of its own. Often the very strangeness, to Westerners, of their personalities causes Americans to characterize them as shiftless, irresponsible, dishonest, ungrateful and a hundred other adjectives denoting inferiority. Obviously for middle-class Americans to work with sympathy and understanding in such an environment requires the deliberate acquisition of a relative attitude toward culture. The alternative is contempt covered by a mask of charity.

Do Americans have any right to thrust themselves into distant societies so different from their own? In the past the United States, like other great powers, has taken that right largely for granted. The idea that there is an American destiny to intervene in the affairs of others is deeply rooted in the culture, even though the United States has never made an attempt to win a worldwide empire. One has but to review the history of American relations within the Western Hemisphere, or in Asia, or the history of church missions, or, indeed,

of America's vigorous and often violent wes
pansion to the Pacific, to find this predomina
our society. American interventions, from
Platte to the Mekong Delta, are a matter of re..
moments of isolationism and retreat into Fortress Amei-
ica have not obscured. Not all interventions have involved U.S. troops. Some, like Crossroads Africa and the
International Voluntary Service, have been pace-setters
for the Peace Corps. Others, originating in the gray
areas of government which lie beyond public scrutiny,
have suddenly surfaced from the shadows in disaster,
like the Bay of Pigs invasion of Cuba. Still others, equally
clandestine but less spectacularly disastrous, have top-
pled regimes from Guatemala to Iran to Saigon. Though
the term "Manifest Destiny" was abandoned many years
ago, the thrust behind it was never more manifest than
during the Presidency of Lyndon B. Johnson, who took
office in the Peace Corps' third year.

The motives that have impelled America's interventions in the affairs of others have been varied and, often,
unacknowledged. Some, like the Marine forays in the
Caribbean of half a century ago, have been crassly economic: the collecting of U.S. bank loans. The political-
military rationale for American cold-war ventures like
the Bay of Pigs and Vietnam is familiar. Other forms of
intervention have been for professed ethical reasons, as
with the saintly, guilt-ridden efforts of Christian missionaries to stop people from eating each other in
Borneo. The mixture of morality, self-interest and self-
delusion that has characterized so much of this intervention — and which is a clear warning to such a venture
as the Peace Corps — is easily discerned in the foreign

policy of President Woodrow Wilson. In *We Give to Conquer*, a critique of American aid, Asher Brynes cites this description of that great idealist and great meddler: "In a program of moral imperialism President Wilson placed the weight of the United States behind a continuous, sometimes devious effort to force the Mexican nation to meet his ill-conceived specifications. Though he oozed sympathy, good will and idealism, his basic misunderstanding of the main elements of life in the southern republic brought disaster in its train."

The Peace Corps is a new form of American intervention. Any opinion of the Peace Corps is bound to be colored, therefore, by one's opinion as to the legitimacy of American intervention in general. Is it part of the American power fantasy to assume that we should — or can — direct the modernization of the world, when this inevitably would mean imposing or promoting American qualities of mind and spirit along with American technology? Whenever the United States sends people or money into another society, the act is tinged with imperialism, however mild. Questioning the purpose of American efforts abroad can be painful; the Peace Corps experience has forced many to do just that. Volunteers have asked, on occasion, if there is really a difference, except in degree, between dropping napalm on Vietnamese to convert them to our form of politics and dropping Peace Corps teachers on Africans to convert them to our form of education. Though the question implies greater conscious intent than the Peace Corps had in its early days, it nonetheless indicates a searching appraisal of national goals.

Two extreme answers will show the range of this issue. One extreme would be to justify the imperialist mission — to update "the white man's burden." The other would be to avoid any form of intervention in other nations.

"The white man's burden" argument says: since our way of life is clearly the best and the *right* way, it is our duty to transmit it to the less fortunate parts of the world. The method involves sending the money and the teachers and the experts to convert them to our way — using, that is, all the tools by which the rich can induce the poor to do or think what the rich want. Often, such peaceful imperialism leads to a more aggressive form. Crusaders are notoriously willing to stick their swords into people who resist the benefits being offered them.

The other extreme, complete American withdrawal from the world abroad, is loaded with its own obvious absurdities. Human questions, in fact, seldom yield to such simple answers as the two extremes we have suggested. American intervention in the third world cannot be halted. Americans are part of the world dialogue. If the Peace Corps is disbanded, other and more massive forms of governmental intervention will remain and so will the still more important intervention of private interests — missions, trade, exploitation of natural resources by American corporations.

The underdeveloped world is under continuing assault as well from the other wealthy nations. Almost all the areas where the Peace Corps operates were once under the colonial rule of European powers. Though formerly colonized nations are independent, they frequently continue to maintain an ambiguous relationship with their former rulers. The armies are gone; but the

European culture remains. That culture, particularly
when its intervention is expressed through education, is
generally assumed to be a "good" influence on "back-
ward" peoples. But, on closer examination, that intervention often begins to appear irrelevant to the people's
needs, at times absurd, even harmful. Peace Corps volunteers have been forced to view this sort of intervention at
first hand in many nations. They have found, time and
again, that things are not what they seem: that often,
indeed, they are the opposite of what they seem. One
example from the Peace Corps experience, admittedly
an extreme case, illustrates the strange realities that can
exist under a veneer of good intentions when people
of one culture intervene in the affairs of another.

In an African country, a former French colony, the
Peace Corps sent girl volunteers to work in adult education centers for women. The centers supposedly teach
illiterate women to speak, read and write French, to do
simple arithmetic, and to acquire some basic notions
of nutrition and hygiene. Most of the students are wives
of local officials, themselves literate, and some earn a
living trading in the local market. The centers are in
small towns, and each is run by an educated African
woman and a girl volunteer. To the visitor, the center
seems comfortably disorganized and cheerful with the
bright colors of African dresses; some women are nursing babies in class. The picture is an attractive one.

Now let us see what goes on in the center. The African
teacher is conducting the class; the volunteer is assisting her. The class is reciting an arithmetic lesson, in
French. The women's voices drone softly: "two plus two
makes four," "five plus four makes nine," "nine plus

eight makes seventeen." Then one woman answers: "two plus two makes seventeen." What's that? She says it again. Look at your paper! Before her the woman has a sheet of paper on which she has carefully drawn the arabic numerals: $2+2=4$, $5+4=9$, $9+8=17$. The woman looks down at the paper, and then she says it a third time: "two plus two makes seventeen." The African teacher corrects her sharply and moves on. But the volunteer wonders. That woman is one of the better students, and the class has been on the same arithmetic lesson for weeks now. Besides, she sells yams in the local market. How can a market woman, of all people, say that "two plus two makes seventeen"? If she did it in the market, she'd go broke in no time.

Exactly, but she does not do it in the market. She knows perfectly well that two and two *yams* are four *yams*. In fact, she can calculate a lot faster in her head than either of her teachers, and she rarely makes a mistake — certainly not the kind she made in class. But in the market she is adding the yams on which her living depends, and she is doing it in her head, and she is working in an African number system that is based on five rather than the Arabic ten. In class, she is doing something entirely different. She is reciting a lesson she has memorized. She has learned to repeat the French phrases for "two plus two . . ." etc., and a couple of the phrases have become confused in her memory. The phrases have no numerical meaning, so she does not realize her error. She has also learned to make certain scratches on paper with her ten-cent ballpoint pen. She makes them very neatly, but she does not see a link between the "4" on the paper and the spoken foreign word for "four", nor between either "four" and four yams. Neither the scratches on the paper, nor the recited foreign phrases, have any connection with the real arithmetic of the marketplace. Similarly, she distinguishes between her written name and her "real" (spoken) name. She recites and writes her lessons because that is what the teacher tells her to do. It is how the Europeans do it. She is not unhappy. She came here out of curiosity, or to be with her friends, or because her husband said to come. Certainly she did not come to learn arithmetic, at which she is already skilled.

The African teacher makes no effort to bridge the gap between market arithmetic and written base-ten numerals. Her job is to make the women recite the lesson properly. Neither she nor her students are stupid, but they are acting out a foreign ritual that has no relevance to their lives. The host government does not appear to care either. If the men running the agency that set up the centers were concerned with teaching arithmetic, they would do it in the local language and they would begin with the difference in number systems. (Amazingly few of the foreigners involved are even aware that this number system, like many of those in Africa, is based on five.) Whether that would serve any purpose is questionable: do the women students have any need in their lives for the ability to write base-ten arithmetic?

The true purpose of the centers is to provide the woman with some of the outward symbols of "modernity." Courses are taught in French in defiance of all apparent sense because the French language is the prime symbol of modernity in nations once ruled by Paris. To the French and to many of the peoples they once ruled it is well known that God, who is competent in all languages, speaks French by preference. In some centers, a course inaccurately called nutrition was popular. It consisted of learning to prepare and serve a meal in European style: separate plates instead of the common bowl, on the table not on the floor, utensils instead of hands; and a couple of "European" dishes. A capable and charming African teacher listed as her greatest success the European meal served by one of her students; she described it in great detail. Nothing in this feat had the slightest nutritional value, but it was of great importance to the woman, as the teacher realized. Her husband will no longer be ashamed of her: he can show off to his friends a wife who can cook and serve like the Europeans.

In retrospect, the absurdity of what was taking place in the women's centers is evident. With the complicity of both "Westernized" Africans and Europeans, the women were being offered the illusion of progress instead of its substance. Instead of whatever useful changes the West might have to offer, the women were given (and wanted) some of the status-conferring patina of the industrialized West: some writing on a pad, a few words of French, a European meal. To Americans, it is doubtless easier to detect the faults of others' interventions than of their own. (The volunteers in those centers, we should note, tried with some success to make their teaching less irrelevant, but they had no control over the curriculum.) In the following chapters, we will see time and again how volunteers, and the Peace Corps itself, have been forced to search out the underlying meaning of their interventions overseas.

To return to the Latin American site where three

volunteers established a co-op, it is clear that American values were imported into the town. The volunteers set out to work a fundamental change. In building a cooperative to supply fertilizer and an improved power source to Indian farmers, they grasped the problems of the day as they saw them and decided to do something concrete. The vague language of diplomatic agreements and legislative enactments did not restrict their decision to intervene. The three volunteers were the kind of people who would have felt uncomfortable in *not* doing something for others born less blessed with opportunity than they. None of the three seemed anxious to bear the "white man's burden." They did not manifest that cool sense of superiority, that aloofness, which too often separates the philanthropist from the philanthropized. Yet in assisting the Indians of the town the volunteers demonstrated a narrowness of cultural vision which prejudiced their efforts. In the first place, they did not make a thorough study of the town. They believed that an agricultural co-op was needed regardless of local circumstances. Had they done their research, they would have discovered that two of the town's mestizos had interests that were being threatened. Had they studied the potential membership of the co-op they would have discovered an almost complete lack of managerial ability. Further, they would have learned that a tractor was far too sophisticated a piece of machinery to be maintained by Indians whose only previous motive power had been their hands. They would therefore have been able to anticipate the amount of training in accountancy, literacy, cooperative management and mechanical skills that would have been needed to get a rather complex agricultural cooperative off the ground. As it turned out, the volunteers had to carry the whole weight of the co-op on their own shoulders. Thus they inadvertently found themselves carrying — if not the white man's — at least a Peace Corps burden. While the Indians may have obtained some momentary benefit from the co-op, the pattern of their lives was not changed from the centuries-old habit of depend- ence on and subservience to a dominating outsider. In fact, though the volunteers scarcely realized it, they had stepped in and filled the role of *patron* in this new endeavor, thereby providing yet another demonstra- tion to the Indians of their inability to function without a beneficent and all-powerful master to dictate the con- ditions of their lives.

In the headlong early days of the Peace Corps, the ambiguities of intervention troubled few if any of those involved. The issues of foreign policy seemed much simpler in those days. There was good and bad in the world, and the American mission was to use the na- tion's awesome power to combat the bad and help the good people who needed help. Young Americans could do both through the Peace Corps. They were a kind of "good seed" to be sown overseas. In 1961, then-Senator Hubert H. Humphrey said that the Peace Corps "is to be a part of the total foreign policy of the United States . . . to combat the virus of Communist totalitarian- ism." Secretary of State Dean Rusk added, rather crypti- cally, that "to make the Peace Corps an instrument of foreign policy would be to rob it of its contribution to foreign policy." The Peace Corps, it seemed, was to win cold-war votes for the United States, but by some undefined methods differing from traditional diplomacy and military action.

The early view of the volunteers' contribution to the people among whom they were to live was best expressed by a Carmack cartoon that first appeared in *The Christian Science Monitor*, then was reproduced in the influential 1961 Colorado State University Research Foundation study of Peace Corps possibilities, *New Frontiers for American Youth*. The cartoon shows a crew-cut youth with a determined but slightly vacuous expression striding out across the globe in the direction indicated by a sign which says: "BATTLE AGAINST HUNGER, INEXPERIENCE, AND APATHY." In his hands the cartoon figure, labeled "U. S. Peace Corps," is carrying standard American hand tools: shovel, rake, pitchfork, square, saw. One thing was certain: this husky youth in work clothes was going to start out by building things and mucking about in the soil. It was almost as though this American were some kind of god who must return to the earth periodically to replenish his vitality. But how was all this to help the people of the third world? Were Americans to take over all the world's underproductive farms and replace all its hovels with split-levels? The Carmack cartoon seemed to suggest this. To a potential volunteer who did not have the ability to use the tools represented in the cartoon, and most did not, the Peace Corps looked to be an undertaking far beyond his skill. For the official of the Peace Corps who had to make decisions about priorities in assigning volunteers, the agency appeared to wallow in confusion between the problems of building things and the problems of human organization. For the citizen of the third world, this U. S. Peace

Corps giant might represent the threat of a new coloni-
alism — an attempt to reconstruct replicas of America
abroad. The cartoon was titled, "To Wage a Better Kind
of War." It predicted with unconscious accuracy the
ironies and ambiguities that would confound the Peace
Corps.

Sargent Shriver's policy of rapid expansion, and the
easy optimism of the agency's founders, propelled the
Peace Corps feet-first into hundreds of exotic situations
in those first years. Americans are impressed with size,
and the Peace Corps itself seemed to be driven by a need
to have as many volunteers as possible in as many places
as possible. Each of those places was the site of an experiment in American intervention.

Soon results began flowing into Washington from
those experiments. The greatest source of internal criticism in the Peace Corps from the beginning was the volunteers themselves (a source denied AID, for wasted
dollars do not complain). Highly motivated and prone
to question authority, the volunteers were vocal in their
criticisms of what the Peace Corps was doing. More
than anyone else, it was the volunteer at the grassroots
who questioned the premises of American intervention
in the third world. Shriver himself encouraged wide-
ranging criticism of everything and everyone, including
himself. An important channel of volunteer opinion was
the Division of Evaluation, which sent critically-minded
men into the field to interview volunteers and bring
their opinions to the attention of the Washington bureaucracy.

The rapid growth of the Peace Corps was the target of
widespread volunteer criticism under Shriver. In the

Philippines, Ethiopia, Colombia and Nigeria, the number of volunteers quickly grew from a few dozen to more than seven hundred. Many volunteers who watched the number of fellow volunteers multiplying around them felt that too many Americans was actually a liability to their mission. That many volunteers, they felt, was too heavy a foreign presence, too much intervention in the nations that were their hosts, too much competition for the largely nonexistent jobs into which they had been sent. This was one criticism to which Shriver turned a deaf ear. Only when Jack Vaughn succeeded him in 1966 did the Peace Corps begin to slow its rate of growth.

The internal debate over numbers of volunteers is helpful in placing the Peace Corps in its perspective as a minor part of the American intervention overseas. Peace Corps people argue whether the agency has too many volunteers in, say, Nigeria; yet the presence of seven hundred Americans, none of them on missions of violence, fades into insignificance compared to the vast network of private and governmental operations abroad. By all the available quantitative measures, the Peace Corps is a very small component of the United States' foreign policy. The total annual budget of the Peace Corps would only run the Defense Department for half a day.

By 1967, Peace Corps volunteers were feeling that, as a voice of America abroad, they were drowned out by the bullhorn roar of other American voices — notably those speaking for military power. Whatever the volunteers had to say in the third world was a whisper; questions raised by war had reached deep into the Peace

Corps and had begun to make headlines. For the Peace Corpsman who took seriously the job of creating more life options for the people among whom he was living, the role of America as preserver of world order, by force if necessary, held many horrors. Volunteers around the world had since the beginning been asked to explain their country's failings, not only in the South and the urban ghettoes, but overseas. Volunteers are not required, as a condition of their employment, to give "official" answers. Most volunteers answer critical questions honestly. Sometimes this has meant expressing total disagreement with U.S. foreign policy. But for many volunteers, disagreement is not enough. Their questioners quickly point out that the Americans with builders' tools have far less strength than the Americans with money and weapons.

The word peace mingles ambiguously with the warlike word corps in the title of the agency, yet rolls off the tongue with surprising ease. Peace, it has frequently been said, requires not only an absence of armed conflict but also the presence of some standard of human dignity. Every culture promotes its own standards of decency. The development of the Peace Corps, as an expression of American standards, parallels almost exactly in time the development of the war in Vietnam. Thus, as an expression of peaceful intent on the part of the United States the small, unspectacular achievements of the Peace Corps have been overshadowed by the doings of the Defense Department.

Volunteers overseas live with an increasingly aggressive image of the United States. Their innocence tends to fall off them in great chunks. Volunteers have worked during periods of violence in such places as India, Pakistan, Nigeria, Cyprus, and many parts of Latin America (not forgetting the Dominican Republic). They are not notably tolerant of the patient, weary lectures of older men like Eric Sevareid, who tell them it's time they learned that peace and war are merely different sides of the same coin. A growing number of volunteers, after their two years' Peace Corps service, are being drafted. They are thus gaining experience of two diametrically opposed experiments of their nation in intervening in the world.

A dramatic dilemma of American civilization has walked onto the stage of the 1960s. Shall it be the Peace Corpsman, symbolizing independence, self-reliance and autonomy, or the soldier, with his tools of coercion and destruction? Or shall it (or can it) be a mixture of money, know-how, coercion and subversion, depending on local circumstances? The dilemma is not only a dilemma of power. It is also a dilemma of purpose.

chapter 3

THE PEACE CORPS IN TEACHING

"In most societies for most of recorded time, education has been a reactionary force rather than a progressive one," Adam Curle of Harvard has written. "Education, often closely associated with religion, has tended rather to hallow antiquity than to promote innovation."

The basic purpose of schooling has been to transmit an approved way of life to the next generation — to make sure, that is, that children behave the way their elders want them to behave. Though they are also learning various kinds of skills, the children are constantly being guided toward accepted beliefs about how people should live their lives. In a traditional or religious society, children memorize the instruction of the Koran or the catechism. In an American school, the children get "citizenship" (i.e., proper behavior) grades. More important, their behavior is influenced by all sorts of "messages" they get every day in the classroom. For example, in *Culture Against Man*, Jules Henry describes the unspoken ways in which American children are taught to compete rather than cooperate. In the United States, a society that accepts a rapid rate of change, education also changes rapidly, though the schools are usually found toward the end of the line of march rather than in the lead. But in the traditionalist societies of the third world, school generally is the "reactionary force" described by Adam Curle.

An agent of change thinking along Curle's lines might well have hesitated before venturing into education in other countries. No such reservations deterred the Peace Corps. From the first days, education has been by far the agency's biggest activity.* For the first five years, more than half of all the volunteers were assigned to some form of teaching. Only in 1967 did the percentage of volunteers in education drop below half, to 48 percent; since the Peace Corps was growing in size, this meant the number of volunteers in teaching was still increasing. Their assignments were varied: they worked in primary schools in Jamaica, in universities in Peru and Ethiopia, in educational TV and physical education in Colombia, in adult literacy in Guatemala and the Ivory Coast. More than half of the teaching volunteers were in secondary schools. Among the continents, Africa has gotten the largest number of Peace Corps teachers, Latin America the fewest.

These patterns were set in the earliest days of the Peace Corps, prehistoric times in terms of American un-

---

* By "education" we mean organized schooling, not learning in general. Learning is of course a central theme of all Peace Corps assignments.

derstanding of the third world. Americans .
deal to learn — more accurately, to unlearn
are still in the dark ages. Peace Corps officials
mon with other Americans then and today,
strongly in two ideas. One was that education of
any kind is good. The other was "education for de
ment," the idea that schooling is the lever of econ⌣mic
progress in the third world. Officials in the countries to
whom the Peace Corps was offering volunteers seemed
to share these beliefs about education; busy expanding
their educational plants, they were prone to ask for
teachers. The State Department looked on approvingly.
Embassy officials overseas are preoccupied with youth;
they spend a lot of time worrying whether the young
elites are being infected by Karl Marx and Mao Tse-tung
rather than trying to assess the depth of youth's concern
for its own problems. Maybe the presence of Peace Corps
teachers would convert the locals to a belief in the two-
party system.

Perhaps a more decisive American myth influenced
the early rush to schools. Especially in Africa, the American sees the foreigner as somehow cannibalistic — dark,
dangerous, and motivated by animal urges which are
hard to predict. Schools, recognizable centers of Western incursion into this cultural jungle, are places where
the volunteer might be able to land on his feet. Schools
are more associated with "civilization" than with the
Heart of Darkness. They are safer. Any American who
has traveled abroad will recognize that the fear of the
"primitive" blows away only slowly, after the traveler
discovers that he can step out of safe American havens
into a new culture and not be eaten alive.

Teaching was also the easiest job for the Peace

Corps to take on. In a centralized school system, the job is standard throughout the nation, so the Peace Corps could plan for large numbers of volunteers with little effort. Teaching seemed the best, if not the only, job for these hordes of liberal arts college seniors who were applying to the Peace Corps. They had no professional skills: they couldn't plant a crop or set a fracture. So let them teach, Washington decided, and this was less an insult to the teaching profession than a manifestation of the view that education is intrinsically good: where the need is so great, any teacher is better than none. For much the same reasons, applicants who had no skills tended to ask for teaching positions.

The volunteers went into training in June or July, got a few hours of practice teaching — if they were lucky, for many never faced a class till they got overseas — and in September of each year the skies rained volunteer teachers all over the underveloped world. In the capital, the staff gave them their up-country location, and a few days or weeks later the volunteers passed through the school doors and confronted the principal, their fellow teachers and, most important, their students.

It happened thousands of times in hundreds of schools in dozens of countries, and it has been quite a confrontation. The variety among local people and circumstances was great, but the newcomer was always an American, usually young, and eager to help. It is touching to try to re-create the volunteers' expectations as they passed through those school doors. In their minds' eye, as they recounted it later, they had expected an austere classroom full of children as eager to learn as the volunteers were to teach. How could the kids not be eager? These countries were poor and illiterate and, with

the end of colonial rule and the revolution of rising expectations, the children were being offered the chance
to be the builders of a new society, to lift their people
out of the ancient cycle of poverty and sickness and ignorance. The hope of a better future lay in these students. All they needed were the tools that education
could provide. The volunteers would bring them the
knowledge of the rich, industrial United States — even
if they were teaching English, for language after all is the
key that unlocks knowledge. Those were the expectations against which the reality of Peace Corps teaching
must be measured.

Class turned out not to be what the volunteers had
expected. Instead of students eager to learn, they found
students eager only to pass the examination by memo-
rizing all the possible answers. Rote learning — the
mindless repetition word-by-word of the text — is the
rule all over the third world. Almost anywhere, you can
hear pupils reciting phrases whose meaning escapes
them, often in a language they do not understand. The
students learn to repeat the words; the content does not
matter; nor does the system ask (or want) the student
to reason. Standardized examinations, over which the
individual teacher has no control, are also common.
When the volunteers tried to vary from rote and the
rigid syllabus, the pupils howled in protest. They had
been taught to memorize — what right did the foreigner have to demand something else of them? "Sir,
what kind of teacher are you? You will destroy us by not
permitting us to pass the examination." Usually the
headmaster or principal upheld the students. He himself
was raised on rote.

For the volunteer in his classroom, the issues that

mattered were specific and immediate. Like most people who are working rather than studying, the volunteers' interests became local and pragmatic; their concern was with *their* schools and *their* students. "My principal is an idiot" was a more important consideration to them than the theoretical underpinnings of Washington policy. If you're a volunteer in a secondary school your situation has characteristics in common with volunteers all over the world. Your students are mostly adolescents, often of widely varying ages in a single class, and, especially if you're new to teaching, you are preoccupied with discipline. Some volunteers faced classes of seventy pupils, and student loads of five hundred. All five hundred were used to local teachers whose tool of persuasion was a whip. The volunteers' nonviolent American methods were misunderstood, and the class was in an uproar. To a young American, everything was strange: the curriculum, the language, the attitudes of both pupils and other teachers. Shaping young minds is a glamorous mission, but teaching, the volunteers found, is largely the grinding detail of preparing lesson plans and marking papers and, particularly if you are teaching beginning English, endless repetition in the classroom.

Reality outside the classroom, the volunteers found, also bore little resemblance to the picture they brought with them from home. Instead of austerity — the "mud-hut image" of the Peace Corps — some volunteers found themselves eating high off the hog, higher in fact than they had at home. "I never had it so good, and I won't have it this good when I go home," one teacher said frankly as she sat in her comfortable living room while her servant prepared dinner. That was in Africa. The idea had been that volunteers were to live on the same scale as their local counterparts, but it turned out in many cases that the counterparts lived very well indeed, because their living patterns had been set for Europeans rather than Africans. In the ex-British colonies, the volunteers found that the secondary school was a compound, literally walled off from Africa; town was often several miles away. The volunteers were assigned to a comfortable house, with a servant, inside the compound. "We're not volunteers," a teacher said in Nigeria. "We're contract teachers, the same as those who come here from Europe under contract to do the same job. We just have a lousy contract — that's the only difference."

Most of all, the volunteers discovered the elites of the nations in which they were serving. From Illinois, all Nigerians looked alike, and so did Filipinos and Bolivians. Up close, though, the volunteers found their new societies to be deeply divided, more deeply than their own America. On one side were the great mass of people, poor and illiterate; that was no surprise. But the ruling class — the small group of the "educated elite" who ran the schools — were far from the eager innovators of the volunteers' vision. The schools were the stronghold of the elite, and many of their traits shocked the youthful volunteer with his democratic, innovating spirit. They were, with individual exceptions, a class of overprivileged rulers, more concerned with cars and other material goodies than with progress, holding the masses in profound contempt; often they were lazy, irresponsible, corrupt or callous. The elites were above all fearful of change, and this fear permeated the schools they ran.

In one of the more enlightened corners of Latin America, volunteers were assigned to schools run by a lay Catholic organization largely controlled by old-line, diehard conservatives. One school director told his volunteer teacher: "These peasants are children. We have to take them by the hand, lead them toward the light, and endow their souls with magic." One method of magical endowment was to make the students perform a certain quota of meaningless labor each day — like digging holes and filling them up again. The volunteer, deciding to leave the burnishing of souls to the other teachers, left the school and went to work with the students' parents.

In thousands of such episodes, the volunteers were finding that there is a lot more to education than mastering such skills as English or mathematics. The cultural complexities of education are acute in ex-colonial countries, as we saw in the case of the women's centers described in Chapter 2. Two cultures are present and at war with each other in the schools: the traditional culture and the "Western" culture imposed by the colonial rulers. The conflict is most obvious in Asia and Africa, but it exists in much of Latin America, between Indian and Spanish in church as well as in formal schools. In the colonies, school was the main instrument of European cultural conquest. An example was the French colonial school, where Oriental and African children recited the famous textbook line: "Our ancestors, the Gauls, were tall men with fair hair and blue eyes." Absurd as this now seems, it illustrates the inner truth that colonial education literally deprived the children of their ancestors and substituted the Europeans as the source of all culture. Nor did this change with independence, for the colonial school had done its work all too well. Even today, volunteers teaching English in Africa get a text which makes the pupils recite: "Our faces are brown from the summer sun." The departing rulers left in power an educated elite that had been taught to despise their own heritage and worship the culture of those fair-haired Europeans. It was this educated elite that greeted the volunteer at the door of the school.

The colonial schools were also monstrously irrelevant to the needs of the nation. Today they are still turning out Europeanized clerks. The curriculum still comes from another world, and the textbooks make Dick and Jane look good by comparison. In one part of Africa, vocational students follow the syllabus of the Guilds of London; they build fireplaces in 120-degree heat. In countries that desperately need better farmers, school teaches children to despise agriculture, and manual labor is a form of punishment. The message of the school is that education is how you get into the elite, and that means high status, high pay, and little work, all in an office. Secondary students in parts of Africa and the Middle East, the volunteers discovered, let one fingernail grow long to prove that they do not work with their hands. This is not "education for development," many volunteers felt, but antidevelopment.

Such were the ambiguities that became evident to many volunteers plunged into school systems in the third world. The subjects they taught were varied, but one staple of the Peace Corps has been the teaching of the volunteers' own language. English, called TEFL (Teaching English as a Foreign Language), is taught by volunteers on three continents. In many nations it is clearly a useful enterprise. However, the teaching of English in the former French colonies of Africa has been a subject of controversy within the Peace Corps. Though it involves only a few hundred teachers and is far from typical, the case of French Africa illustrates the complexities with which the Peace Corps has had to try to grapple. On the scale of national needs in these countries, English ranks close to the bottom — and the needs ahead of it are massive and neglected. English is in the secondary school curriculum only because that curriculum was copied from France. Only a rare student taught by a volunteer will ever have a chance to use English, assuming he remembers what little he learned. A world language is useful anywhere, but these countries already have French. The students are overloaded with languages: French, their school language, is often a third or fourth tongue for them, and most African students are still having trouble with it. In Guinea, volunteers tried to teach English to kids who were failing other subjects because of poor French, and who were falling asleep in class because they didn't get enough to eat. In most of the secondary schools in this region, the majority of pupils will drop out, and even those who graduate can hope for at best a low-level clerical job.

When a volunteer teacher in Togo told his class that "with English and French you can go anywhere," the class answered back: "Who's going anywhere?" The students, in touch with the harsh reality of their country, knew with a clarity denied the ebullient and already-mobile volunteer that most of them had little hope of going anywhere in their lives, either in Togo or outside.

The Peace Corps rationale for sending English teachers to former French colonies in Africa illustrates the sort of often unspoken American cultural values that underlie the agency's decision-making. Present, of course, is the assumption that volunteers are probably useful even if this cannot be proved, as well as the belief in education as intrinsically good, "education for development," and a preoccupation with youth, particularly elite youth. "It *must* be good to have our volunteers in there with those elite kids," a Peace Corps official once said as her only response to criticism of the French Africa operation. In this case, we also find what we may call "English language imperialism." The notions involved here are: learning English has a moral value, because you can read Thomas Jefferson and John Stuart Mill and absorb a *good* culture (i.e., our own); it would be handy if all the world could communicate in one language, and it would be particularly handy for us if that language were English, rather than Esperanto or, God forbid, Chinese.

Within the Peace Corps, the purest expression of this point of view came from Harris Wofford, former Director of the Ethiopia program (and, it should be noted, one of the agency's most courageous innovators). In a talk entitled "English as a Language of Learning and Law," Wofford said: "Now let me . . . suggest that the teaching of English is the single most important thing that the Peace Corps does in Ethiopia or in Africa." He hailed Ethiopia's decision to make English its language of higher learning, and he went on: "When Ethiopia has fully arrived in the twentieth century . . . it will certainly have its disagreements with us, but the disagreements will be in our terms of discourse." (Note that "our." It refers to Americans, not Ethiopians. An Ethiopian might not be so charmed by the prospect that disagreements with the Americans will be in what to him are foreign terms of discourse.) Wofford raised his sights: "Let me shoot higher — a long shot. English may well be the best language for twentieth-century development. . . . You can't be well read in English without learning something about due process, equal protection of the laws, freedom of speech and self-government." It was indeed a long shot. Today Ethiopia, tomorrow the world!

Science teaching, in contrast to English, has been a generally happy enterprise for volunteers. Here American values are useful, for the pragmatic, mechanical bent of most young Americans is probably better suited to science than to any other subject. In most third-world classrooms, science is taught by rote out of a book, and nearly always the book itself is foreign. Students rarely if ever have a chance to work out a principle with their hands, or to see in the real world an example of what they are studying. Products themselves of a nonscientific background, where natural events are explained by theology, they are offered science through texts whose examples are taken from Europe rather than from the world outside their doorsteps.

Even a volunteer who is not specialized in science can usually do better than that. Many have instituted field trips in their schools, so that students for the first time can see in their own familiar world tangible illustrations of scientific principles. Others have designed simple experiments using local materials, providing their students with their first experience of working scientific experiments with their hands. In Tanzania, a volunteer teaching elementary physics brought ice from his kerosene refrigerator into his classroom and let the students watch it change from solid to liquid. Simple: but no one else did it, and those students had never seen water in its solid form. The scientific approach laps over into other subjects. One volunteer, using *The African Queen* in a literature class in the Cameroons, suddenly realized that half his students had no idea what a boat was or, therefore, what the story was about. After that, he devoted time to the study of boats, bringing photographs of different kinds of ships into the classroom.

In some cases, volunteer teachers have a chance to teach these simple methods of conveying science to local teachers. In India, volunteers with no science background have successfully conducted practical workshops for Indian science teachers. Allen Bradford, himself a volunteer teacher in India, reported on the volunteers' workshops:

With a few tools and a UNESCO sourcebook, they are teaching high-school teachers how to build demonstration models for science classes using cheap native materials like bamboo and string. The science teachers gather for this special training in batches of fifteen. The workshops last ten days apiece.

The workshops clearly fill an educational need. Science equipment manufactured by Indian companies is of poor quality but usually not cheap. A store-bought skeletal model of a frog, for example, is twelve times more expensive than the cost of a workshop experiment that removes the skin of a real frog with acid. At the

workshops, teachers learn how to make such basic apparatus as a fulcrum . . . they also learn to stage action-
oriented experiments that will hold their students' attention.

Unlike some earlier Peace Corps educational efforts,
the workshops do not conflict with "the system." The
demonstration equipment and experiments are based
on the syllabus for grades 9-12. The workshops are able
to emphasize a different approach — a practical approach
to science aimed at capturing the students' imagination
— without making a frontal assault on the system.

Conflict with the local "system" was a problem, as
Bradford suggests, in most Peace Corps operations: volunteers were at odds with the established way of doing
things. As the Peace Corps grew, sheer numbers of volunteers in a school system created its own set of problems. This was especially true of the Peace Corps secondary school programs in Africa. On the assumption
that, if one hundred volunteers in a country are good,
six hundred are six times as good but not six times as
hard to plan and administer, the Peace Corps literally
swamped the schools of some countries. By 1965, Nigeria, Ethiopia and Liberia were crawling with volunteer teachers. (By no accident, two of these nations were
also leading American client-states in sub-Saharan Africa.) Nigeria had the biggest group of Peace Corps
teachers in the world: 570 in 1966. Ethiopia had 500 in
1966, with an extraordinary 180 in Addis Ababa alone.
In Ethiopia, volunteers constituted a third of all secondary school teachers, and the staff spoke at one time
of increasing the total to over 1000. The Philippines

actually began to reach for that number — 800 in 1962.

The volunteers' importance in the school systems of such countries was cited by the Peace Corps with pride. But flooding the schools with teachers created a dangerous dependence on the Peace Corps, whose goal was making countries *less* dependent on outsiders — Americans as well as ex-colonials.

Numbers were also a distinct handicap to the volunteers. In cities like Addis Ababa, the volunteers retreated from the Ethiopia around them into a stifling Little America of their own making. "Our biggest problem is each other," was a common remark where volunteers were found in groups. In Cameroon a volunteer teaching in a missionary-run school, all of whose staff, like himself, were white, commented acidly that "this is the first time I've lived in an all-white community." The more time the volunteers spent with each other, the less they spent with the local people, the less they knew about the country and — though this was not realized at first — the less effective they were in the classroom. The temptation to retreat from the local scene affects all volunteers, of course; having other young Americans around just increases the odds that the volunteer will take the easy path.

From even the most troubled of teaching programs, the majority of volunteers have gone home relatively happy with their two years. Armed with their American optimism and faith in education, they have found their satisfaction in their own performance and in the struggle for existence overseas. If that performance was less than outstanding, it was often better than that of the local teacher against which the volunteer compared himself.

And if the struggle to exist was much easier in an elite school compound than the image of hardship the volunteer saw when he applied to the Peace Corps, getting along in another culture, even in a superficial way, was always a challenge to someone who had never been out of middle-class America. As a result, most teachers report (in the questionnaires filled out when they finish their service) that they believe they were useful and that they would do the same job over again.

Where the living was particularly easy, volunteers usually were able to rationalize the difference between their home-and-servant and the mudhut they had expected. Interviewed in the field, these volunteers came up with ingenious explanations to justify the way they were living. A favorite line of reasoning went: the elite will make the decisions about this country's future, and to gain the elite's respect we have to live like them. Maureen Carroll, an early Philippines volunteer, found these reactions when she returned there in 1966. "Although their students represent all levels of society, the volunteers live, work and socialize mostly with their professional and middle-class peers," she wrote. Miss Carroll also found that: "In many cases the style of volunteer living has changed dramatically from the early days of the program, when most volunteers lived in small rural barrios. . . .

"The recurrent volunteer remarks to me about their living conditions ran the gamut in tone from guilt and discomfort to justification and defensiveness. 'We've really got the easy life here in the Philippines. . . . I didn't live so well at home. . . . I've got an air-conditioned bedroom. . . . After all, these people we're living with are Filipinos, too. . . . They're the potential agents of change; they need our support and encouragement. . . . I can't communicate with a fisherman. . . . That hut business is just a lot of image anyway.' "

In the little African nation of Togo, Peggy Anderson, another volunteer teacher who returned later to the scene of her service, found that the volunteers tended to reduce their ambitions to fit their situation. They were teaching English, which many of them did not feel was a high-priority need in Togo. Most were living an elite life, having little contact with average Togolese. Only an exceptional few of the teachers had succeeded in climbing the barriers between themselves and the Togolese — they were learning the local language and getting to know their communities. Some had moved out of their European-style houses.

"But the average volunteer is not so lucky, or so resourceful," Miss Anderson reported. "Instead of seeking the experience he expected, he accepts the experience he gets; instead of changing his situation, he changes his objectives. By the time he goes home, the original goals have vanished.

"Everybody will leave a few friends, they say as they depart, and in that claim lurks the greatest irony of all: volunteers who shudder to hear the Peace Corps called an instrument of American foreign policy or American propaganda are satisfied — *are satisfied* — to go home knowing they have made some friends for America, even though they can see that that is of virtually no use to Togo."

Not all volunteers were satisfied with such justifications for their presence. As the Peace Corps involvement in education grew, an articulate minority of volunteers began to question the value of what they were doing. Skepticism was found, especially in those countries that have a combination of widespread illiteracy and over-developed school systems. The schools produce more graduates than the economy can employ and, because the dropout rate is high, they turn out droves of half-educated people who refuse manual labor and yet are qualified for nothing else. "Educated unemployment" is common in India, and in Nigeria, hundreds of thousands of dropouts are decaying in the cities. (More accurately, they are "pushouts": primary school graduates who could find no place in secondary schools.) These unemployables, whether they are pushouts or the graduates of the secondary school system, are ripe for brainless revolutionary movements. Rotting in urban shanty towns, bitter because they missed the elite gravy train, these lost youths are more prone to respond to the appeal to hatred of a Hitler than to, say, the self-help appeal of a Julius Nyerere of Tanzania. Without just this class of marginal citizen such senseless conflicts as the one in Cyprus might never have generated much steam. Some volunteers began to ask whether the Peace Corps, by its support of these very school systems, was not merely helping to produce a class of citizens whose only visible potential is for atavistic and autocracy-prone conflict.

The financial cost of this kind of education is as exorbitant as the social cost. Uganda not long ago was spending "around two percent of [its] Gross Domestic Production providing secondary education for a little over one percent of [its] 14 to 17 year-olds." * At this rate it would cost more than Uganda's total domestic production to provide secondary education for everyone. And all that to accomplish what Hanson calls "education for frustration." The Peace Corps, in sending volunteers to teach in such countries, has laid itself open to the charge that it is implicitly encouraging the ruling elite to spend lavishly on an irrelevant school system while starving the nation's other needs.

As ex-volunteers and staff members brought back descriptions of what was going on overseas, the Peace Corps decision makers have begun to take another look at their original conception of their role in teaching. Their reaction was remarkably fast, in terms of history, especially bureaucratic history. At first the agency simply accepted what was then an unchallenged view of education. Others are still trying to transplant their systems unchanged to other societies. In a few short years, the Peace Corps has moved ahead of them in its thinking. The Peace Corps strength lies, not in the ability to avoid mistakes, but in the willingness to learn from its own experience and to discard its own preconceptions and those of the experts.

That size in Peace Corps operations is not always an asset had become increasingly obvious to some officials. Like dinosaurs eating themselves into extinction, the huge teaching operations were visibly sagging under their own weight. The numbers in the Philippines, an early field for wholesale broadcasting of volunteers, were

* Quoted in *Imagination and Hallucination in African Education*, by John W. Hanson, an excellent study published by Michigan State University.

cut back drastically before being allowed to crawl back up to the present total of eight hundred. In 1966, the Africa Region of the Peace Corps embarked on a new policy toward both numbers and teaching in general. Washington also decided to de-emphasize the teaching of English in French Africa. This decision was reached after two years of internal debate; by contrast, French and other foreign agencies sending English teachers to that region have *never* to our knowledge seriously questioned the value of what they were doing.

In the big African teaching programs, the trend by 1966 was to hold down the number of volunteers. Coincidence played a part in this change. The Ethiopian Government, seeing its landscape overrun by young Americans, cut back its requests. Nigeria was a more painful case. Despite all sorts of efforts by volunteers as well as staff, the teachers there were still living in isolation from the African environment. Nigeria's internal troubles also devalued its status as the world capital of Peace Corps teaching; in the 1967 civil war, volunteers had to be evacuated from Eastern Nigeria. Far from dreaming of ever-greater numbers, Washington was coming to wish it had not gotten so deeply involved in Nigeria's schools. More important, the Peace Corps had dropped teaching as its priority goal in Africa in favor of what it called "rural transformation."

Washington began to put more stress on the importance for teachers of community involvement. Shriver had stated this principle as far back as 1962: "We're not sending people overseas who want to be only teachers. . . . A teacher whose role is restricted to the classroom is like a fighter with one hand tied behind his back." But this ideal remained largely on paper in the

early years, perhaps because it was often seen as motivated by considerations of foreign policy: the hand tied
behind the back was only the hand of friendship. Nice,
but not important. The volunteers were in an environment where community involvement, whether it meant
getting acquainted with peasants or fraternizing with
students, was viewed by their host-country colleagues as
distasteful and perhaps vaguely threatening. Many volunteers responded to any criticism of their position with
the cult of professionalism: they were there to teach, and
time spent on community involvement would only detract from their primary purpose. Host-country officials,
when Peace Corps staff proposed measures designed to
promote the volunteers' local involvement, were baffled
if not offended. Who wants to hang out with peasants?
And why learn about a primitive culture which we are
trying to destroy through our schools? But the Peace
Corps clung to its belief that a teacher who did not
know his students' culture could not be effective in the
classroom.

Despite various forms of opposition, the Peace Corps
has made considerable progress on this issue. Austerity
has proved to be the strongest force that can push teachers toward community involvement. To some, Peace
Corps austerity is simply polishing the "mud hut
image" for the sake of Congress and the American public, and others see it as a repellent way of moralizing
about the Puritanical virtues of service-in-poverty; but
in fact austerity has a hard pragmatic justification. The
only way to understand how people live is to live as much
as possible the way they do, and in the third world, that
means living poorly (if you identify with the people
rather than with the elites). Accordingly, Washington

has been cutting volunteer living allowances, taking away vehicles provided by its early mother-hen administrators, and in many places the agency has tried to get teachers housed in the local town instead of in the school compound. Some volunteers have howled, but in general these changes have been accepted with good grace. Ironically, the loudest howls — and in 1966 the threat of a strike — came from the teachers in Nigeria, who until then enjoyed what was probably the highest standard of living in the Peace Corps. (What the Peace Corps has come to consider "too high" a standard of living is often considered too low by others, especially other Americans overseas. Depending on the local cost of living, volunteers get from $50 to $175 a month plus housing. Another $75 a month is banked for them at home.)

But in the walled-off schools of Africa and the elitist universities of Latin America, there is considerable question whether the goal of community involvement, as now defined, can in fact be attained by the average volunteer. So far, at least, he has not done it. The barriers that separate school from community seem to be too high for any but the exceptional volunteers to scale. One alternative, proposed by many volunteers, is to define the "community" as the school itself. Volunteer professors in Latin America hold that there is plenty to do on campus without plunging into the slums, and a teacher in Africa, viewing the anarchy in his school, may say that reform begins at home. But the students themselves were born outside the walls, in another culture, and the teacher volunteer who does not understand that world is hardly qualified to promote reform on campus.

Beyond this, the Peace Corps is only beginning to face the fundamental issue of whether it is worthwhile to send volunteers to teach in an irrelevant school system. When Washington began to realize what the schools do to students, the first reaction was to go along with the volunteer's own rationalizations. If he was doing a good job in his class, it was argued, his pupils were benefiting, and maybe other teachers would emulate the volunteer. Changes wrought by volunteers in their schools — and there have been many changes — were cited with pride in Washington, with little thought to whether the changes would outlast the volunteers' presence, or spread to other schools, or, indeed, whether they were worth two years of his time. Great stress was laid on the volunteer's activities outside class: starting sports teams and school libraries, or doing something worthwhile in summer vacation. At the very least, the volunteer was a "good seed," and, if the soil seemed rather flinty, no one had yet proved that it was totally barren.

Recently a new and more radical school of thought has appeared among a minority in Washington. In the view of this group, the "new purpose," as some of them call it, of the Peace Corps in teaching should be to concentrate on educational reform. Sending volunteers just to fill teaching slots is not enough, unless they are in a position to be agents of change. In assigning volunteers, preference should be given to those jobs in which they can have the greatest effect on the educational structure. While this group does not oppose the standard secondary classroom jobs that are the staples of Peace Corps teaching — where it hopes they will motivate reform by their example — it is far more interested in assignments in which the volunteer's influence can be multiplied. One obvious example is teacher-training institutions, where the volunteer can bring his American methods and attitudes to hundreds of future teachers who in turn will teach thousands of children. Another favored assignment is primary and pre-primary schools, because the system here is usually far less rigid than in the standard secondary school: the children have not yet been so thoroughly beaten into the rote-learning mold.

The "new purpose" is an advance over traditional thinking, and it is shared by some third world leaders, most notably Tanzania's Julius Nyerere, but it carries its own set of dangers. Its proponents have understood the role of education as a conveyor of culture. They want the culture that comes off the conveyor belt into the students' minds to be different from what is now being loaded on. These are not old-style missionaries seeking to impose a rigid dogma on helpless pupils. Their cultural imperialism is a mild variety whose goals — problem-solving, democracy, creativity — are positive values in *American* eyes. Yet it does not take too great a leap of the imagination to visualize the new purpose taken to an extreme. Then we would hear the schoolchildren of the third world reciting to their approving volunteer teacher: "Our ancestors, the Founding Fathers, were democrats and innovators. . . ."

In many ways, the Peace Corps recently has been groping toward a clearer view of what it can and cannot do in education. From the first fuzzy view of education as a general need in the third world, the agency is moving toward a more sophisticated knowledge of the school systems of individual nations and the problems and possibilities it can expect to find within each of those systems. Peace Corps officials have begun to distill out some of the lessons implicit in the experiences

of the thousands of volunteers who have taught overseas. Two of those lessons can be seen in the following
individual cases.

In Nepal, a single volunteer helped to modernize the
nation's science teaching curriculum. He did this, not
by teaching in a school, but by working in the bureaucratic maze of the Ministry of Education. The volunteer
was working for a Nepalese official who had been educated abroad. It was the Nepalese, not the volunteer,
who made the decision to reform the science curriculum.
The volunteer was merely supporting that decision with
his efforts and, perhaps, with his foreign prestige. The
will to change had already been shown before the volunteer arrived. By contrast, a Peace Corps official warned
against any effort to get into curriculum reform in a nation where the local educational leadership showed no
desire for such change. There is, he wrote, "no surer way
to get convicted of cultural imperialism than by a blun-
dering onslaught on a system you do not control."

In Peru, a girl we shall call Carmen taught in a remote Indian village. Carmen was the first person to teach
third grade in the school, which previously offered only
the first two grades. Her performance is described in
a Cornell University report on the Peace Corps in
Peru:

She introduced a number of innovations in the Cuyo
Chico school. She began teaching music — the scale,
which her pupils liked to sing, games, rounds, dancing, etc. She began decorating the classrooms and installed a bulletin board. She began employing visual aids
. . . as well as teaching in ways unknown to the area
previously. Another volunteer . . . cooperated by mak-

ing microscope slides of human blood to show the children. . . . Carmen took her pupils outside to measure things while they studied measurement. She took them on nature hikes, and had them make stone ovens to roast potatoes. She introduced a puppet theater to induce her reserved pupils to talk. The local teachers simply talked in the classroom, so pupils had no form of non-verbal reinforcement in their lessons — nothing to see, feel or touch. . . .

During the summer school vacation which is normally a period of serious regression in level of learning on the part of rural Indian students, Carmen organized a three-week summer school. Only six students attended in the beginning but attendance had built up to twenty-five at the end — no mean achievement in a rural Indian community where parents highly value physical work.

Carmen's innovations filled in gaps rather than replacing existing methods. Like the science teachers in India, she did not come into conflict with a local "system." Her teaching techniques carried less of a cultural or ideological freight than, say, those of a history teacher in a secondary school. The effect of Carmen's presence was to increase the opportunities of both her pupils and her fellow teachers.

Carmen was an exceptional teacher, and the volunteer in Nepal was in an exceptionally lucky situation. The great majority of Peace Corps teachers have not had either her skill or his luck. On the whole, however, they have acquitted themselves surprisingly well. Going into difficult classrooms in school systems they did not understand, and usually without ever having faced a class before, most volunteers have performed at least adequately. If teachers like Carmen are rare, so are the outright failures.

Nonetheless, the Peace Corps experience indicates that the agent-of-change role is especially difficult and dangerous in teaching. Promoting the boiling of drinking water, for example, may involve a volunteer in the complexities of social change, but he is at least seeking a well-defined goal. The volunteer promoting boiled water deals with cultural problems only as they affect that primary goal. In the hazier field of education, however, changing or preserving the culture itself often seems to be the goal, so the volunteer is necessarily thrust into a much more sensitive area. Another danger is that almost any teaching situation gives the volunteer too much power. In most of the Peace Corps jobs we discuss in the following chapters, the volunteer deals with adults who are free to accept or reject what he has to offer. Even if they accept the goal of boiled drinking water, the people rather than the volunteer will determine what forms of cultural change they will undergo in order to achieve the goal. School is different. In that closed institutional setting, the pupil, whether he is a primary schoolchild or a student teacher, has little liberty in his confrontation with the volunteer. This power inevitably tempts the volunteer to what one Indian called "the smuggling of cultural values under the cloak of education." The difficulty of determining whether a teacher is really providing something useful to his students or just "smuggling cultural values" is perhaps the most basic problem facing any agency intervening in the schools of another society. That question has been raised, but not resolved, by the Peace Corps experience.

chapter 4

THE PEACE CORPS IN
RURAL ACTION

Food is the central, overwhelming problem of the third world. Most of the people of this world do not get enough to eat, and most of those who eat enough to stave off hunger lack some essential foods, notably protein. Hunger has always been the companion of life in the poor countries, and until recently Americans generally assumed that, though things were pretty bad over there, at least they were gradually getting better. It has become painfully obvious that this is not so. The food supply per person in the third world is declining, and there is every reason to believe it will continue to decline under present conditions. In India and in many parts of Latin America, people have less to eat today than their parents had. As population grows at an ever-faster rate, agriculture is falling farther behind. In countries that are primarily rural, the failure of agriculture is bound to block national development. The gathering food crisis is commanding the attention of the United States Government, which finds its farm surpluses vanishing into food relief, and in a few years food supply seems certain to be the preoccupation of those involved in aid to the third world. So far — and this too is a central fact — the overwhelming majority of efforts to improve agriculture in the third world have failed, and those few successes on the record have occurred under circumstances that usually cannot be duplicated elsewhere.

The Peace Corps interest in food production has grown considerably in recent years. In the early days, only a handful of volunteers were put into agricultural jobs. By 1967, 1350 volunteers — one-tenth of the total — were working in agriculture, one-third of them in India alone. Another 2500 were classified under the catchall term "rural community action"; more than half of these were in Latin America. Even the Peace Corps in Africa, then mainly in education, decided in 1966 to give first priority to what it called "rural transformation."

But the Peace Corps attracts few applicants with farm backgrounds, and fewer still with agricultural expertise — their numbers are in any case relatively small in the United States. The liberal arts graduate who is the foot soldier of the Peace Corps is usually an urban- or suburbanite who has never seen a spread bigger than a windowbox, and knows only in theory that milk comes from cows rather than bottles. Most of the volunteers working in agriculture are just generalists with three months of training as their only preparation for the jobs they are supposed to do.

Despite their lack of farm skills, some generalists have found a useful role for themselves in what we call "rural action." Under this heading we include all attempts to increase rural productivity, mainly farming, but also livestock or fishing or forestry, and related efforts such as cooperatives, road-building or farmer education. The content of rural action cannot be separated from community development, and it is intimately related in many cases to health (both subjects to be taken up in later chapters). Our emphasis, in treating rural development separately, is on the productive processes involved in rural areas.

Peace Corps opportunity in rural action lies in the special nature of agricultural development in the third world. The rural volunteer travels from the city where his airplane lands out into a remote village that may take him several days to reach. Though new to the volunteer, this is the age-old environment of village life in a traditional society. Each village differs in its terrain and customs, its problems and prospects, but some constants apply to almost every place that rural volunteers serve in the third world. Life is self-contained within the village limits. The villagers know little about the world outside, often including the next village; outsiders are usually the subject of deep suspicion. In return, outsiders know little about the village; no one was able to tell the volunteer much about it before he went. As we have seen, in the secondary school the elite is well represented — in person and in tradition — but in the village the elite is represented at most by a few low-level officials whose influence is weak. Village life, the volunteer discovers, is regulated by an all-pervasive local culture. To a

much greater extent than in America, the individual vil-
lager is subordinated to the group and must on pain of
social disapproval obey its detailed rules of behavior.
Even farming methods are part of the culture. A farmer
in Iowa can switch crops or machinery without undue
fear of reprisal from the keepers of his own local culture.
Not the traditional farmer in the third world. For him
to innovate, to change his farming methods, is a radical
and daring act, much as if the Iowa farmer announced
he was going to vote Communist or take up polygamy.
Land farmed by those age-old methods yields barely
enough to keep the family alive, and yet, the volunteer
soon finds, no one has any sure idea how to increase
those yields. These are people whose options in life are
few and whose power over their environment is limited.

"You are thrown onto the edge of Asia. Life is very
slow there and plenty real," a rural volunteer wrote.
Community involvement comes naturally for the rural
volunteer, unlike the teacher in the elite school who
must scale the compound walls, against the rules of the
system, in order to reach the local community. The rural
volunteer has no such problem; he is plunged right into
his new environment. In many cases he finds himself
living in a mud hut — the mud hut of the Peace Corps
image — because that is the only housing in the village.
He eats the local food, not because he cannot afford better, but because that is all they sell in the market. He
does whatever the local people do for entertainment —
talk, usually, maybe an occasional dance — because the
village has no movies or bars. Often he goes to bed at
dusk, because there is no electricity and his kerosene
lamp is broken. There is no one to talk to but the vil-

lagers, and, since they are not going to learn his language, he must learn theirs. Life is harsh and boring. If he isolates himself from the village, the rural volunteer is likely to find the monotony intolerable, and seek either a transfer or a ticket home. If, on the other hand, the volunteer can make the life of the village his life, if he can find his satisfaction in what he is doing in that community, he can find a useful job for himself and at the same time live his life with considerable gusto.

The successful rural volunteers soon become aware of the complexities of rural action. Making farms yield more food involves dealing with a whole set of apparently unrelated factors, ranging from pesticides to politics. The first set of complexities deals with farm technology. Rarely is it possible to raise yields by a single change — for example, by introducing a new variety of corn that gives a higher yield. Almost always, a single change will give little result unless other innovations are made at the same time: fertilizer or pesticide in addition to new kinds of crops; new farming methods and often new tools; more water, which means irrigation. To complicate it further, any given "package" of innovations is only of local value. Because of variation in soil and climate, what works in one place — the proper blend and dose of fertilizer, say — will not work somewhere else, even in the next village. Yet these technical problems are only the beginning. A farmer who rarely sees any cash at all cannot buy fertilizer or seed or tools unless he has credit, and in most places credit either does not exist or is only offered at loan-shark rates — frequently 100 percent interest for six months — or is tied to what the lender is selling, which is not fertilizer.

A yield higher than the family can eat is of no use to the farmer unless he can sell it. This means a market is needed, and a road to that market, and a means to transport the crop at reasonable cost. Some aspect of new farming methods may also collide with the local culture in ways that the outside technician cannot understand. For example, in many cultures livestock has prestige value that outweighs its cash value, so cattle are kept instead of sold. Further, the farmer cannot successfully adopt new methods unless he gets continuing, rather than one-shot, advice on, say, how and when to apply fertilizer. Nor can he use fertilizer successfully unless it arrives in the right amounts and the right blend at the right time of the year. This involves the ruling elite, for it is the government ministry in the distant capital that must order the fertilizer, make sure the roads are repaired, and see to it that the truck arrives on time. Land ownership also involves the ruling class. In most of Asia and Latin America, the farmer is a sharecropper exploited by a powerful landlord. He has little reason to improve his farming, since the landlord will take away most of any gains he may make. Higher yields, therefore, must wait on a drastic change in the pattern of land ownership or the conditions of tenancy. Since the landlords are part of the existing establishment, and the tenant farmers are not, any real land reform is equivalent to social revolution.

In order to achieve higher farm yields, a development program must move on all these fronts simultaneously. It must also reach out to communicate with millions of farmers scattered in thousands of remote villages. The demands in manpower and institutional structure are extremely heavy: agricultural extension agents, men to run field trials of new farming techniques, cooperative organizers, men to operate new markets, road builders and a score of other new occupations. Most important is the village-level worker, as he is called in India, the man who is the indispensable link between the village and the resources of the outside world. Because of the endless variety in local conditions, all those involved in rural action must be innovating men capable of improvising solutions on the spot. Yet these are precisely the kinds of skills that the underdeveloped nations lack. Short of technically skilled people of all kinds, these nations have still fewer people who are motivated to be rural agents of change. Almost everywhere, anyone with education flees the hinterland for the bright lights and modern status of the city. As we have seen, the attitudes of the local elite make them peculiarly unqualified for rural action, in large part because of the rote learning, distaste for manual labor and elitist outlook which they acquired in school.

This has been the Peace Corps opportunity. Although it cannot supply skilled agronomists in any number, it can supply one need: people with modest skills and high motivation. The very attitudes lacking in the local elite are common among most volunteers: willingness to learn and improvise, to work without a book of rules, and, more subtly, respect for traditional village culture which the elite may consider "primitive." Under the right circumstances, rural action often turns out to be a new sort of paradise for the city boy who, a few months before, did not know his muck from his milch.

Such an opportunity presented itself to the Peace

Corps in Niger, a desert nation in West Africa. There the farmers grow peanuts to sell and millet to eat. They use only the simplest of hand tools. The thin soil, watered only by a brief rainy season, yields meager crops. The impression prevails in Niger, based on very sketchy research, that the soil could produce more with fertilizer, animal-drawn plows and different planting methods. Two dozen volunteers were assigned to Niger's rural development agency, which is commissioned to bring about rural change on a number of fronts. It is supposed to sell fertilizer and equipment; to provide credit by setting up farmer cooperatives; to set up and manage markets; and also to set up small village stores to sell essential goods. All this action is supposed to happen out in the villages, far from the capital. The volunteers were assigned where the action is, usually in pairs, with a couple of the agency's men, who, like the volunteers, were typically young and ill-trained.

In one instance, two volunteers were working with two local men of the agency who happened to be exceptionally competent and interested in their work. When we visited them, we found the four men working together on a demonstration vegetable garden — all four laboring with their hands, a startling sight in a society where the educated shun any manual effort. Breaking off his efforts, one of the volunteers took us on a protocol visit with the chiefs. The whole village establishment — a dozen middle-aged and elderly men — lay sprawled under the shade of a baobab tree listening to a transistor radio. The volunteer explained the role of each in the village's extremely complex power structure. Each activity related to production fell under a different chief: one looked out for water, one for land rights, one for livestock, and so on. Any agricultural project had therefore to be cleared through all the chiefs whose jurisdictions were involved; if one chief was not consulted, the project was sure to fail. That evening, beneath a kerosene lamp in the volunteers' two-room adobe dwelling, one of the volunteers, Mike, talked about his experiences. The peanut shellers the Niger development agency had been promoting among the local farmers were simple, hand-operated machines; their purpose was to enable the farmer to bring his peanuts to market already shelled, lightening the burden on his donkey or camel. Fully half the shellers went out of order within a year after the farmers got them, Mike found. Many only needed a bolt, but nobody had any bolts, not even the government agency. Farmers ignorant of any kind of machinery had no idea what was wrong with their shellers. A local official (who reputedly detested whites) had cooperated freely with Mike in seeking a solution to this and other difficulties. "I asked him what I should do," Mike said. "He told me: 'You're the first white who ever asked me — the Europeans were always *telling* us what to think.' "

In another Niger village, so remote that it lies beyond nowhere, the volunteers' first assignment was to find some way to help in the market where the farmers brought their peanuts to be weighed and sold. They soon discovered that the middlemen who weighed the crops were systematically cheating the peasants with short weights — a time-honored practice in markets all over the world where European or local traders deal with peasants. So, moving in on the problem like Re-

form Democrats in New York City, the volunteers prepared a plan to eliminate cheating. They presented it to
the village leaders. The market men and their friends,
who together made up the village's power structure,
voted down the New York-style reform that would have
cut into their own income, and the volunteers quickly
realized their cause was hopeless. Not only had they run
head-on into the power structure, but they also discovered that the peasants had no feeling of being cheated
— the weight (and therefore the price they were getting)
was what they had always gotten. If the volunteers had
pushed the issue, they would have so alienated the local
decision makers that they would have been unable to
get support for any other projects — and the peasants
would still have been cheated. They quickly dropped it
and turned to other ideas: demonstration vegetable
gardens, and organizing a group of villagers to dig a
much-needed well — both projects that were strongly
supported by the power structure.

By his third year in the country, another volunteer,
George, had become well known in the village, where he
attended all the local dances and weddings. Like many
another foreigner, George had often wondered why
women hauled water for miles on their heads instead
of using the many donkeys which are idle most of the
time. One day he saw for the first time a woman leading
a donkey bearing four jars of water, in contrast to the
one jar she could have carried on her head. George made
a point of congratulating the woman and telling other
villagers about it. Weeks later, at a wedding, the local
praise singer inserted in his plaudits of the newlyweds
an embroidered version of the incident, repeating what

the volunteer had said. By using a donkey to haul water, the woman had gone against custom, risking the community's disapproval. By backing her with his prestige, the volunteer strengthened her status and improved the chances that other women might emulate her.

In a somewhat larger community, big enough to have an elementary school, another volunteer started a school garden and got the pupils interested in cultivating it. The garden had several purposes: introducing new crops, providing food, showing the pupils that agriculture need not be despised as an occupation. The volunteer found these elementary school children to be more willing to work with their hands than the students at the nearby agricultural school, which trains agents for the Niger development program. These older students had already picked up elite attitudes and despised manual labor.

What strikes the visitor about these rural volunteers in Niger is how happy most of them are. Among the volunteer teachers in the elite schools, by contrast, you hear a lot of complaining about "lack of intellectual companionship." They get bored with their polite, aimless conversations with the local elite, with whom they share few common interests. "What is there to talk about?" they ask. But the successful rural volunteer rarely makes this complaint. The difference lies not in him but in the two situations. Unlike the usual teacher, the rural volunteer is involved in action. He does not just chat with the villagers, he talks with them purposefully about common goals they have come to share: they both want that well to be dug. In one village, there was a Yalie whose passion was flying; here he could not even fly a kite, and no one could discuss Paul Goodman with him, but he was not complaining. He had moved beyond merely intellectual interests into action.

The volunteers' contribution to the Niger development agency is being increasingly recognized by officials. A striking example of this occurred over the proposed reorganization of Niger's cooperatives. An official from the main office called together all the volunteers in one region to tell them about his reorganization proposal and to pump them for their experiences with the cooperatives. As a result of what the volunteers said at this meeting, the agency drastically altered its plans. The agency man noted later that volunteers living in the villages knew far more about his cooperatives than he, living in the capital city. "I spend half my time reading the reports I ask the volunteers to write," he said. "That's how I find out how my plans are working out in practice. They've also given me some excellent new ideas."

One volunteer produced a potentially important technique for protecting the farmers' interests in the reorganization. The farmers are cheated when their crops are weighed, because, being illiterate, they can keep no record of weights, nor can they inspect the weighers' records. The volunteer developed a system of accounting using symbols — drawings of familiar containers — which illiterate farmers could understand. When the agency required that crops be recorded in these symbols on the weighers' records and on cards held by the farmers, the farmers for the first time had the means to protect themselves against cheating.

Rural action is a heartbreakingly slow process, and neither the Peace Corps nor Niger's rural development agency has "transformed" the bush. But they have perhaps made a start on the beginning. The agency works a little better because its leaders are better informed. A few people have tried productive innovations, and a few of these may survive and spread. Some local people have been exposed to the volunteers' inventiveness and optimism and respect for manual labor; some of their attitudes may take root. The volunteers have collected a great deal of information on their villages which will be invaluable to those who follow them. Such are the modest measures of success in rural action. It is nothing a public relations man could photograph. It is so intertwined with other factors that, if Niger's farmers take off into a more productive life, no one will be able to say just what part the Peace Corps played in it.

Other cases from the Peace Corps experience illustrate the endless variety of prospects and problems that confront volunteers in rural action. In a small African nation, volunteers were assigned to what were billed as farm schools: settlements to which rural youths were brought, allegedly to learn better agricultural techniques. The school's management was hopelessly bad. In one fiasco, the school invested large amounts of money in irrigation wells, and actually succeeded in harvesting fewer potatoes than peasants a few yards away were getting with traditional methods. All efforts by the volunteers to improve the schools were blocked by the management. In a neighboring country, the hens of a volunteer who was trying to start egg production were commandeered by the local governor and served up to the president of the nation: a clear case of living off capital. Another poultry volunteer had better luck with a governor's appetite. Though the nation called itself socialist, this governor's capitalistic greed was aroused by the poultry project. He cooperated fully with the volunteer — and took some of the eggs to black market them across the border for his personal profit.

Direct economic ventures by volunteers have raised the question of what to do when the people of the country lose money by following the volunteers' advice. In teaching, the loss due to an incompetent volunteer is real, but cannot be measured in currency; in some rural programs, the loss can be counted in hard cash. In Guatemala, for example, volunteers induced farmers to join a cooperative to raise rabbits; when this poorly planned venture failed, the farmers were out the money they had invested. So far the Peace Corps has not faced this question. Nor, of course, have the governments of the third world. If their agricultural development agencies give farmers bad seed or poor advice, it is the farmer who suffers the consequences, while the agency's employees continue to draw their salaries.

Diversification of earning power has often been urged as a method of rural development. In many localities, native arts and crafts are already highly developed and present a chance for tapping a large tourist or export market. Some of the Andean countries of Latin America have managed to mount programs to stimulate village handicraft production, which turn out usually to be ephemeral trinkets at best, gaudy bastardizations of local crafts at worst. Volunteers working in these projects, while not denying the value of the increased income to their communities, nonetheless tend to despise their role as apostles of a junk culture. The markets are with the big tourist outlets. These markets demand conformity to their own idea of design. Volunteers, trying to develop a sense of independence in the people with whom they are working, come to appreciate the integrity of native crafts and are thus torn between culture and commerce when it comes right down to the hard decisions of where and how to market. Few have found a way out of the dilemma that would produce income and at the same time help to revive the ancient Indian culture. Most give in and become, by implication at least, dime-store imperialists.

Cyprus, where for a year and a half before the outbreak of communal warfare the Peace Corps maintained a contingent, presented unusual opportunities for increasing agricultural productivity dramatically by focusing on one key factor. Cyprus, blessed with an extraordinarily mild climate, is excellently situated to export citrus and early vegetable crops to the lucrative European market. The key factor is irrigation water, almost all of which must be pumped from underground wells. Three or four times too much water was being used on the arid island's export crops. Any increase in the efficiency with which water is used will automatically increase the foreign earnings of the country. Establishing where the waste occurred, and demonstrating new ways for saving the precious water, were jobs that the Peace Corps had just begun to tackle when fighting between the Greeks and Turks broke out. All the elements for success in rural action were there; but the forces of history, deeply rooted in tradition and garlanded with romance, proved too much for the Peace Corps and its sponsor in the irrigation work, the UN's Food and Agriculture Organization.

The school-to-school program, a special form of rural action, suffered from several of the ills that beset Peace Corps and American aid generally. School-to-school involves the use of funds raised by a U.S. school or civic organization to put up a school building in some foreign community that is too poor to build one of its own, but is willing to put up some materials and labor. Toward the end of 1963 the Peace Corps initiated a pilot program: the construction of a school in rural Colombia. The idea caught on: the public relations man who did the most to get the idea going was hired, and the Peace Corps said it hoped to put up three thousand schools in three years, or roughly three per day. (The actual total, in early 1966, was seventy-seven.)

Carta Blanca is the name of the community involved. The history of Carta Blanca, and how the Peace Corps came to be involved in it, is as long and involved as a Russian novel, but the essence of the plot is as follows:

In the fall of 1963 a publicist came to Colombia to select a site for a school to be built by donations from the PTA of an elementary school in the United States. The Peace Corps made the following four conditions on the use of the funds raised by the American PTA:

1. The school must be near a jet airport so as to be easily accessible for publicity purposes and foreign visitors;

2. The community must be chosen because of its inability to put up a school of its own;

3. There must be a volunteer, already working in the community, to supervise the building of the school and to keep track of PTA money;

4. The school must be finished in time for a mid-May, 1964, inauguration ceremony involving PTA people and dignitaries from the U.S. Embassy and USIS.

Not wanting to leave anything to chance, the publicist had armed himself with a movie camera when he set off for Colombia. There he picked up a couple of volunteers and soon found just the kind of community he was looking for, a place called El Peligro. El Peligro was poor. The movies would document that. El Peligro was only a short distance from a jet airport and thus could easily be reached by United States dignitaries for ground-breaking and inauguration ceremonies. El Peligro was already an active Peace Corps site. The publicist shot his movies and went home.

Everything seemed propitious: a conveniently located lot was said to be available in El Peligro for five hundred dollars. The village padre and other community leaders were high on the project. Following the prearranged plan, the volunteers in El Peligro made a stab at buying the land, only to find that the owner of the lot was in the hospital. Later, the padre went to the hospital and approached the owner of the lot; five thousand dollars was the price now quoted by the owner, who, being nobody's fool, had already heard that rich gringos were interested in his property.

The Peace Corps, undaunted, began looking for another lot in El Peligro and soon found one, on a less-convenient hillside location, priced at an attractive three hundred dollars. Sold. Two days later the people, already trained in self-help (called *Acción Comunal* in Colombia), had finished digging the foundations. But even as they dug, a villain was plotting to spike their hopes. This villain, one Señor Alvarez, was a local satrap of some misty oligarchical eminence. Alvarez, to keep control of local progress, had sneaked into the hospital and bought the centrally located lot before the decision to move the site of the school to the hillside location had been announced. Alvarez had paid a good deal more than the lot was worth just to keep control of the situation.

Of course, when Alvarez found out that the center of gringo interest had moved away from his land and up the hill he flew into a purple rage, threatened the security of every man in the vicinity, and then hired three of his own men to start building another school on the piece of land he had purchased. Forthwith the community split. Some of the people knuckled under to the threats of the *caudillo*, Alvarez. About half of the community continued with the school building up on the hillside. "It got ridiculous," said one Peace Corps observer, "when we had the Peace Corps brass, USIS, the ambassador, and some volunteers in El Peligro for a dedication ceremony." A showdown came right in the center of town. Alvarez and his boys showed every evidence of getting nasty. And so the Peace Corps, seeing that it had already split the community from top to bottom, decided to pull out.

That was the end of the El Peligro school and the beginning of the Peace Corps education in sending Santa Claus into rural action. But the Peace Corps was in too deep to back out, and it put one of its own staff members on the project to bird-dog it to completion. He found a new site, Carta Blanca. A new start was made, a new spate of difficulties arose and were quickly shoved aside, and finally a lot was secured and ground-breaking ceremonies scheduled for early January. The publicist, back in the United States, needed photographic proof for his PTA constituents that work was going ahead. The ambassador and several USIS types with cameras put in a quiet appearance in town for ground-breaking ceremonies. No mention had been made of the availability of outside funds, but the people of Carta Blanca, unschooled peasants, took one look at the august assemblage and exchanged narrowed glances with each other.

From this point on, the story gets funny, then pitiful. The local volunteer, who had been working quite satisfactorily in the community before the unexpected and gratuitous school-to-school bonanza hit, gradually began to sense the community's loss of initiative and pulled out to devote himself to other neighborhoods in the area in which the spirit of self-help still remained intact. Everything was dumped on the hapless Peace Corps staffer, who was forced to take over the job of ordering supplies, canvassing the community for transportation, and wheedling and cajoling the people of Carta Blanca to turn out for work parties so as to get the school done on time. The staffer found himself alone like the Dutch boy with his finger in the dike. Reports had it that at one point this staff man, whose job is to support Peace Corps volunteers, was to be found standing in the mess of the partially completed school bellowing to the oblivious hillsides in an effort to frighten the peasants into showing up for work.

School-to-school began to look like another American mistake in foreign aid even before the people of

Carta Blanca confided to the volunteer that they could no longer see their way clear to working on their school for free, but must be paid by the Peace Corps. And if anyone's eyes were not opened when this happened, they should have been opened when the people followed up this confidence with a gracious offer to come down to the half-completed shell of the school and fake a half-hour of work for the movie men.

The school in Carta Blanca was still not finished six months after its scheduled inauguration, despite an additional cash infusion from the embassy. However, just over the hill, in a neighborhood unblessed by the presence of either a volunteer or of school-to-school, the people of the community had built a school similar in size to the one projected for Carta Blanca. They had built it in six weeks without help from outside, and this was a community every bit as poor as Carta Blanca. Why? Because they wanted it. They knew no one would provide it for them.

Needless to say, volunteers were bitter about an intrusion which divided a community rather than united it, and which had the effect of killing off a Peace Corps site without so much as providing a completed school building (at last report it was still unfinished) as a *memento mori*. One got the impression that the people involved — the Peace Corps, the publicist, the PTA, the big industrial concern that loaned the publicist to the Peace Corps to get school-to-school started — had little idea of the destruction that can be wrought by giving money away. The goal of getting-the-job-done took precedence over all else, including finding out whether the job was worth doing. The American obsession with education was carried to its final folly: the school building was deemed a good in itself, no matter what, if anything, went on inside it.

The Peace Corps did not sense when it leapt at the PR gimmick of school-to-school, that money giveaways combined with performance deadlines and "spontaneous" expressions of gratitude and international felicity on the part of the recipients belonged back in the dark ages of international assistance. The Peace Corps in this case proved itself insensitive to the needs of Colombia. Dependency and helplessness have been established as character traits in *campesinos* by centuries of subservience to church and *patrón*. Self-confidence can be acquired by such people only by getting them involved in doing something that they can finish by their own efforts. Of course primary education is needed in Carta Blanca. But there is something needed even more, and that is an awareness among the people that they themselves are the greatest development resource that their community owns. This is not to say that all development problems can be solved by self-help methods alone — obviously they can't. The best example is, in fact, schools. An education system costs money and requires huge numbers of trained people — teachers and administrators. No Carta Blanca can go it alone in education for nationhood. What we are dealing with here is the unilateral entry of a foreign power to create only the form — the shell — of education, not the substance. A school building implies long-term commitments on the part of the local community and the national government. The cost of the building will look petty, in thirty years, when all other costs — teachers, maintenance, texts, administration — are totaled. These long-term commitments can be undertaken only by someone with long-term responsibility to the country, not a two-year volunteer.

PTA funds, or any other foreign assistance money, can at best be kept inviolate from graft only so long as the volunteer is there to watch out for it. The best protection against the graft that has riddled so many foreign aid schemes is not a volunteer or any other outsider but a strong sense of independence and self-respect in the people who are the beneficiaries of the schemes. That is the lesson of Carta Blanca.

In its rural action programs, the Peace Corps often gets into an entangling alliance with a much larger source of money, AID. On paper, this looks like a desirable combination. AID has what the Peace Corps lacks: money, equipment and skilled technicians. The Peace Corps has what AID lacks: people willing to work out in the bush where the action is, in places where AID's high-paid technicians refuse to go for more than a whirlwind visit. Cornell's research report on the Peace Corps in Peru concluded that "U.S. aid as such does not necessarily make Andean communities better off" — it describes one massive AID fiasco which clearly left its intended beneficiaries worse off — and it goes on to say that "U.S. aid distributed by Peace Corps volunteers makes Andean communities better off." Certainly this has been true in some cases, but there are others in which the AID relationship has subverted the Peace Corps operation to the benefit of no one. AID's resources have tended to corrupt the Peace Corps, both staff and volunteers, in much the same way as the

PTA money did in Carta Blanca. This is not a hair-shirt viewpoint, and we readily concede that outside resources are usually necessary for rural action. But easily available AID materials obscure a basic principle of rural action: the need for local incentive and competence to carry on after the volunteers leave. A volunteer who has spent months in an unsuccessful effort to get the local authorities to order feed for chickens, and wants to leave more behind than the bones of starved hens, will turn gratefully to the AID man who offers to send a ton of feed up on the next truck — thus relieving the local authorities of any responsibility for their inaction and postponing indefinitely the day they do decide to act. Often, also, volunteers are requested by AID to act as menials in an operation that is pointless by Peace Corps standards; resentful volunteers call this "baby-sitting bulldozers for AID."

Though the Peace Corps is far from being free of political motivation, AID far more frequently ends up playing the next move in great-power chess. Some of its "aid" is no more than cold-war bribery, which cannot be said of the Peace Corps. Even when volunteers are sent to a country because of its political importance rather than because it is a good place for the Peace Corps to work, there is a serious effort to find them reasonable assignments. Possibly one reason for the difference between the two agencies is that volunteers object when they are wasted, whereas money and bulldozers remain silent. AID also has a weakness for flashy projects that have what they call "impact" and can be photographed; the clearest example is the silly and offensive clasped hands symbol that AID insists on slapping on so many of its visible accomplishments. One AID man, whose thinking typifies the cold warrior mentality that has come to invade foreign assistance with CIA-like thoroughness, complained: "Your Peace Corps boys are going to do all the work, and when they're done the Communists will slap their sign on it. . . ." This man obviously did not understand how difficult it is to slap a sign on a human being.

How the Peace Corps can and cannot collaborate with AID is illustrated in one African country that is both an administrative mess and a prime cold-war target. Volunteers in the far bush supervised trials of new corn varieties for AID; they were not agronomists, but the results of the trials were far more valid because they were present. But in this same country some volunteers were also assigned, at AID's insistence, to supervising village oil palm presses designed, in theory at least, to increase the country's supply of cooking oil. This project was hopeless for the basic reason that the government of the country would not pay the villagers a price for the palm nuts (from which the oil is pressed) high enough to induce them to sell. The Peace Corps knew this from its volunteers, but it was snowed under by AID, which cared more about pleasing the African president with a showy project than it did about the supply of cooking oil. The epilogue of that story was that the volunteers were soon withdrawn, and the AID oil presses sit quietly rusting in the bush.

An educational TV collaboration with AID in Colombia paid off, as did a cooperative venture in marketing crafts from rural villages in Ecuador. A bridge-building program started by AID in Nepal (well described by Eugene Mihaly Bramer in his book, *Foreign Aid and Politics in Nepal*) fell through and the Peace Corps got stuck with the fiasco. Each encounter with AID is different, and much depends on the people involved; as a general rule, such alliances are much more likely to succeed when the two agencies' goals coincide (the corn trials) than when they differ (the oil presses).

Looking over these varied experiences, it can be seen that the Peace Corps, while not registering any great number of successes, has begun to define a useful role in rural action. The Peace Corps has learned more than it has accomplished, which puts it well ahead of those many other agencies that have neither accomplished nor learned. Doubtless the volunteers so far have eaten more food than they have caused to be grown in the third world, but this rather dismal thought must be measured against the almost uniform failure of other efforts at rural action.

The emerging role of the Peace Corps, best illustrated in Niger, is to help provide the vital missing link between the village and the outside world. As in most agricultural development programs, the weakest point in Niger is the contact between government services and villagers. What looks good on paper in the capital frequently looks terrible in the bush. The local government agent seldom does anything to remedy whatever is wrong. Perhaps he does not care whether the program works as long as he draws his pay; usually he is afraid to chance a new idea himself or to tell his bosses that their program is failing. But the volunteer does care and he is not afraid — his career is not at stake, and the worst that can happen is that he is sent home. This unique position, not any technical skill, is the volunteer's greatest asset. He can be more daring than any bureaucrat. An Indian official, B. P. R. Vithal, pointed this out to an arriving Peace Corps group. "Whenever his [an Indian official's] performance or motivation falls short of the ideal you have set for yourself," Vithal said, "remember again that it is not due to the fact that he is an Indian and you are an American, but because he is an official doing a job and you are a volunteer on a mission. There would perhaps have been the same difference between you and an American official."

For the Peace Corps to function effectively, it has become apparent, several conditions have to be met, not all of them under the agency's control. The country's rural program has to be in good enough shape so that the small leverage of the volunteers can show results. In one country, volunteers' efforts to promote poultry failed, not because the farmers were unwilling, but because the government consistently failed to supply the necessary feed. In the case of the disastrous African farm schools, the Peace Corps took government promises at face value; it never fully understood how hopeless the schools were. In Niger, on the other hand, the agency was functioning relatively well. Another condition, seemingly obvious but often ignored in practice, is that both local officials and the Peace Corps have to understand what volunteers can and cannot do. The officials in Niger, after four years of experience with the Peace Corps, are able to put the volunteers into jobs that use their talents, rather than requiring technical skills they lack. In India, on the other hand, the Peace Corps rushed in hastily and gave the Indians the impression they were getting "agricultural experts," with results that were unsatisfactory to everyone involved. One Indian official commented that the two volunteers under his jurisdiction knew less than their Indian counterparts about farming. He concluded that the Peace Corps was just a cultural exchange program. He, and other Indians, were less resentful of the volunteers' ignorance than they were of misleading information given them by the Peace Corps when it claimed it was going to supply them with experts.

An additional requirement for successful Peace Corps participation in rural action is suggested by the volunteers' experiences. It is the need for action research on the part of each volunteer sent out into the hinterlands. The volunteer has to study his whole environment to see how the rural system works. No one else will do the research for him. Probably no one else will even be aware of the interrelatedness of the different influences on rural life. One agricultural volunteer took the concept to its logical conclusion. Having spent two desultory years in a remote country with few farm markets and many agricultural problems, he re-enlisted for another two years and struck out into the hills. There he explained his intentions to the village, was given a plot of communal land, and set himself up to farm the plot with only the same tools and resources as the local farmers. Gradually, during the course of his first year, he learned at first hand the nature of the problems faced by the farmers in that area. At the same time, he won their confidence by being able to prove not only his good intentions but the usefulness of the many small innovations which he undertook on the farm. This volunteer said, "There must be millons of opportunities such as this all over the world." He was talking about the opportunity to do original research and at the same time to combine it with meaningful action. In an opposite case, the Carta Blanca school-to-school debacle, a detailed study of a community but a stone's throw away had been published by a distinguished sociologist. This study clearly defined the problems school-to-school would face. Peace Corps officials did not read it.

A Peace Corps successfully engaged in rural action can render a special service to the United States Government. Within the next couple of years, it seems virtually certain, the world food problem will rise to the top of the United States agenda on foreign economic policy. If the past is any guide, we can then expect that Washington will announce one or many crash programs to "save the world from starvation." Nothing is more certain in rural action than that "crash" programs will do just that — crash. It is depressing today to contemplate the energy, funds and goodwill that the United States doubtless will soon expend in not helping to solve the food problem.

The Peace Corps, in its own operations and through ex-volunteers working for other agencies, could offer an alternative to crashing failures. It could be a voice of realism saying: there are no panaceas; rural action is complex and requires tremendous local knowledge; success is the sum of many small and unspectacular actions; and, above all, rural change is slow, very slow. Such voices are already being heard — in the India and Nepal AID missions, for example, where former volunteers with outstanding local knowledge and command of the languages have been hired. But these are isolated instances; bureaucratic change, like rural change, is very slow.

chapter **5**

THE PEACE CORPS IN PUBLIC
HEALTH AND BIRTH CONTROL

The dead you may seldom see, but the sick are all about
you in the third world. The Asian leper in the main street
whose face is half eaten away, the African child's belly
swollen and hair turned orange from malnutrition, the
South American Indian's eyes clouding as the cataracts
grow: these common sights explain why the Peace Corps
has, since its beginning, sought a role in health. By 1967,
some fourteen hundred volunteers, just over 10 percent
of the total, were in health projects of various kinds.

The Peace Corps had only the faintest idea what it
was getting into with its early health projects. No area
is more delicate for the agent of change. Even more
than education, health practices are intimately linked
to the culture in which they exist. Because medicine
deals with the ultimates of life and death, health beliefs are usually part of the larger system of religious

faith. This is symbolized in the figure of the traditional healer (or "witch doctor") who ministers to both body and soul: priest and physician in one person. If the value of the healer's cures is sometimes dubious — though many are more effective than Westerners tend to believe — the healer's role as priest-psychiatrist is nonetheless vital to his community. The agent of change who undermines the healer by imposing a Western medical system is imposing psychological insecurity at the same time.

The technology of Western medicine is not as easily transferable as one might think in viewing the widespread poor health of the third world. Poor health is less a lack of specific treatments than it is a part of the general cycle of poverty; people's health may not respond to improved medicine in the absence of economic growth. An example from American history is the decline in infant deaths in New York City in the first three decades of this century. According to Dr. Walsh McDermott of Cornell University, that decline was associated less with medical change than with "intense community development" and a rising standard of living. Sanitation is often impossible in the third-world environment. When an African woman spends most of her waking hours in the drudgery of hauling water and firewood many miles to her home, she can hardly be expected to listen to the public health worker telling her to waste what she has painfully gathered on a novel idea like boiling the family's drinking water. Nor has Western medicine, despite its sensational advances, produced effective treatments for pneumonia-diarrhea, the biggest killer of infants in the third world.

None of these considerations daunted the Peace Corps. Armed like most Americans with the twin shields of optimism and ignorance, the agency plunged into health as it did into the myriad other problems of the third world. At first the Peace Corps relied on skilled medical personnel, doctors, nurses and technicians, and its efforts were more in treatment (curative medicine) than in prevention (public health). Projects that concentrated skilled people and ample medical supplies on curative medicine were popular in those early days. This approach had succeeded in the United States, so it seemed logical to apply it to the medical problems of other nations.

An example was the T. project in a small African nation. Conceived in 1961, Year One of the Peace Corps, T. was to be a demonstration project. By displaying in a single community what modern medicine can do, the Peace Corps could set a dramatic example that would be emulated throughout the nation.

T. is an African market town a day's journey from the nation's capital. Its streets are crowded and dirty and throbbing with the African zest for life. People live in homes ranging from decayed European buildings to makeshift tin shanties to traditional African thatched huts. Next to the noisy outdoor market is a hospital, the only one for many miles. To a Western visitor in 1961, the hospital looked dirty and sloppily managed. The water supply was forever breaking down, and the male nurses seemed callous in their treatment of the patients. The number of doctors at the hospital varied from one to three. Its resources were hopelessly inadequate to serve a population suffering from the usual list of African diseases, those conveyed by water (dysentery and shistosomiasis), insects (malaria), protein malnutrition (kwashiorkor) and many others.

The Peace Corps arrived in 1962 to remake medicine in T. The first team of twenty volunteers included four doctors; the rest were other medical professionals: nurses and medical technicians. The group represented many man-years of medical training, and it was armed with thousands of dollars in AID drugs and equipment. The volunteers lived together in a compound of European houses; their blue Jeeps became a familiar sight on the streets of T. Though small in number, the medical group was a massive American presence in the hospital, where volunteer doctors outnumbered the locals. At first the volunteers worked only in the hospital, at curative medicine. Later, some of them moved into public health, then nonexistent in T. Volunteers conducted mass inoculations and set up school programs to teach sanitation. In 1964, the first group was succeeded by a second highly-skilled group that included two doctors.

The T. project appeared in Peace Corps publicity, but outside the town itself few people knew what actually was going on there. By 1965, rumors spread that the project was in trouble, that the two volunteer doctors were on the verge of resigning. It was then that one of the authors arrived. The visit was an education in the perils of intervening in the field of medicine.

Drs. Dean and Paul were in fact an unhappy pair. Dean, the official leader of the medical group, wanted to ask Sargent Shriver some questions: "Why was the T. project so badly planned? And prepared? Why were the jobs not more specifically stated . . . the goals clearly

defined. . . . Why wasn't the Peace Corps tougher
with the African government when it didn't honor its
commitments?" But Dean had never discussed these
questions with the Peace Corps staff. Some of the doctors' gripes were more personal. Nurses have a "natural
hostility" to doctors. They complained of lack of "intellectual work"; but under cross-examination, this
turned out to mean lack of professional advancement.
(Some months later, in Washington, one of them was
interviewed about his reasons for leaving. "My work
was of no value," he said. "No value to whom?" the in-
terviewer asked. "To me," the doctor explained.) One
doctor was casting around for reasons not to accept the
U.S. ambassador's rather wild suggestion that he run
the hospital in another town. "Maybe running a hospital as you want is not enough," the doctor commented.
"After all, who wants to be Schweitzer?"

Both doctors felt that people — both Africans and
volunteers — had not been nice to them in T. The tide
of self-pity swelled rapidly in Paul as he described his
reactions to the African community: "Unbelievably
insulting . . . treated like kooks. . . ." And then the
doctor delivered that most classic of Peace Corps statements: "They didn't welcome me with open arms!"

The history of the second medical group under
Dean's leadership, pieced together from different accounts, was a sad one.

Dean had led the twenty-one volunteers into T. in
June 1964. Dean wanted to: assert the group's authority
with the local medical system; force the Africans to
honor their contract commitments; keep the group
united with a common policy; and, naturally, do better
than the first group.

Having been advised by some members of the first group to assert authority quickly, the new team had charged right in to accomplish instant revolution. Dean conceived the idea of requiring *weekly* reports from each volunteer on the changes they had instituted. The unity of the group was, in theory, to be maintained by the frequent meetings at which they voted their policies.

Trouble had not been long in coming. Instead of playing dead, the African medical establishment resisted the American onslaught. The African male nurses continued to steal the penicillin. When a volunteer nurse reported this to Dean, he told her to collect evidence against the African nurse she had observed stealing. Dean then made the charges public at a hospital meeting, without informing either the African nurse or the hospital administrator, and demanded that the nurse's head be served up on a platter. The African nurses had stuck by their comrade and, since some were political appointees and since the hospital needed them more than the volunteers, the Africans carried the day.

Instant revolution did not go over. In many ways, the existing order resisted the Peace Corps attempts at change. In apparent exasperation, Dean had thought up the hairiest of harebrained schemes — a strike! His idea was that the volunteers would walk out — selectively, two or three at a time, for a few days — until the Africans agreed to his demands. The strike never took place, however, that idea being replaced in Dean's mind by the much sounder notion of his own resignation.

The Africans were just as unhappy with the group — especially its doctor leader — as the group was with the Africans. The African view, as expressed by Dr. S., the main local personality at the hospital, and others, was that the group had come in giving orders from the day they arrived. They had made no effort to find out why things were done as they were, but simply assumed that the American way was the right way and that the Africans had better get on the ball. By raising issues publicly, the volunteer doctor had made compromise impossible. His handling of the penicillin-stealing episode had left Dr. S. no alternative but to back the African nurses. (Stealing drugs was and is standard in African hospitals, and there was little that Dr. S. could do about it without risking open revolt and a vendetta by the thief's political friends.)

The volunteers had isolated themselves from the Africans. Dr. S. stressed how this isolation made communication impossible: "Dean never came over to my house to visit so I could never go see him when a problem came up. John [leader of the first volunteer group] and I had our troubles but we could have a drink together in the evening and talk it over till we found a compromise that avoided a complete split. That never happened with Dean."

The public health team included eight volunteers. Their work was part medical and part propaganda. They gave shots and distributed milk and examined babies; they also tried to promote new ideas in nutrition and sanitation. In theory, the medical work was to help the propaganda: school children getting shots and mothers bringing their babies for treatment and weighing were to be captive audiences for lectures on good health practices. Attendance at two public health lectures indicated what in reality was taking place. The first was at an outdoor traveling clinic to which most mothers were bringing their babies for weighing and inoculation. One volunteer was filling syringes, another was weighing the infants. When the mothers got through the line, they were seated on the sand nearby to hear advice on how to keep clean and avoid infection. The nurse lecturer did not know the local tribal language, so she spoke through an interpreter. More accurately, she spoke *to* the interpreter. She and the interpreter stood, set apart from the seated women. The volunteer spoke in a low, hurried monotone to the interpreter; her body was turned away from the audience, and she never seemed to look at the women. The interpreter barked out the Word with the smug grin of the half-educated young African male who has caught hold of the skirts of the establishment. When the lecture was over, the interpreter quickly dismissed the women, who hadn't seemed to be listening anyhow. No questions had been solicited or asked.

The second lecture was given by a volunteer who made posters for the public health people and was described as their best platform performer. She was addressing about thirty men, who sat on benches under a tree while she stood by her Jeep showing with little cutout figures the unhappy consequences of stepping in manure. That same interpreter stood by her. Unlike the first lecturer, this volunteer cast her delivery in the form of question-and-answer. Some of the men knew all the answers and gave them eagerly. There was much laughter when a man scored a bull's-eye. "But," said the volunteer — but they were not putting those answers into practice. The buckets at the well were still sitting on the ground, amidst the manure, instead of swinging from a branch, as she had told them to do. "I said all these things six months ago — and nothing's happened!" the volunteer exclaimed, unable at last to contain her exasperation.

This kind of public health propaganda did not seem effective: the lectures' intended content was different from the messages actually conveyed to the audience. The main message the first girl conveyed was that she wanted to avoid contact with the women (for whatever reason) and did not know enough of their language even to say "hello." The second volunteer expected instant revolution and was irritated when the men failed to perform it. Her audience was motivated to know the right answers — but not to put them into practice; it was a kind of litany.* The interpreter effectively conveyed his contempt for illiterate females and, even with the men, he had the habit of smugly answering questions without passing them on to the volunteer. The first girl rattled off her speech, containing half a dozen revolutionary ideas, at a pace that made it impossible for her listeners to follow what she was saying, much less to put it into practice; one-quarter the speed would have been too fast. Neither girl displayed any knowledge of, or interest in, the workings of the community to which their listeners belonged.

The volunteers as a group were alienated from the community around them. None of the volunteers spoke

---

* Similarly, in the women's adult education centers described in Chapter 2, volunteers have seen an African teacher drink unfiltered water from the tap while leading the women in reciting the lesson: "We must always filter our drinking water." Such episodes do not strike those involved as absurd, because the true purpose of what is going on is the recitation of the lesson, not the act of filtering the drinking water.

the local language and none was trying to learn it. The volunteers' lack of interest in the community matched their ignorance of it. The volunteers showed little sign of having grown as human beings. They were unusually dependent on higher authority. Their effect on African-American relations was summed up in the common accusations of racism and exclusiveness made against them by the Africans.

The volunteers in this project were doing work that had short-term value, but they were not creating anything permanent, and what good they did was bought at a price far beyond the means of the country in which they did it. The hospital volunteers were saving lives, but they were not imparting any techniques or kinds of behavior that would contribute to saving other lives after they left. The public health volunteers were saving lives too — not with their lectures but with their inoculations — and healthier children in that town will bear witness to their presence for years to come. But there was no evidence that they had any effect on the health practices of the community.

The T. project ended less than a year later, in early 1966, when the second group of volunteers finished their terms. The Peace Corps made the decision to kill the project after four years, although the original plan had been to supply volunteers for at least six years. In place of this one-town operation, the country was offered a modest public health project in which small teams of volunteers, with two generalists to each nurse, would be spread around the nation. The Peace Corps decision was neither as easy nor as inevitable as the history of the T. project would indicate. The troubles of the medical group were little known outside the remote area where they were working. The nation's government wanted the project continued, in part at least because it had become dependent on American manpower and money to provide medical care in T. In the interests of smooth international relations, the local U.S. embassy also wanted the T. project to go on. In these circumstances, the easiest policy for the Peace Corps would have been to sweep criticism under the rug and carry on with the original design.

In its last few months the T. project produced a curious and revealing sidelight. Joan, a nurse who had caused much of the trouble in the hospital, had joined the public health group. Finding little to do in the town of T., Joan drifted to a nearby village in search of work. Here there was no hospital, and in fact no outpost of Western medicine in any form. Joan was on her own alone, without a doctor to direct her, without the medical supplies of the hospital.

Joan did what no other member of her group had done — she befriended the village's traditional healer, an older man of great status. Haltingly, with the few words of the language she could use, Joan began to learn about the village's native medical system. Her most important discovery was that the healer's practice was largely restricted to setting broken bones. He did not offer any treatment for the tropical skin sores that were common in the village. Joan knew how to treat these sores, and she knew that they could be treated with materials available in the village. Once Joan and the healer were on good terms, they were able to work out the obvious arrangement: Joan treated sores and referred broken bones to the healer; he in turn sent the sores to her.

Joan's African counterpart was Adam. A semiliterate young dropout, Adam was paid a tiny sum by the villagers to be Joan's assistant. The volunteer passed on her skills and her responsibilities to the young African as quickly as possible. "As soon as I saw that Adam could handle a sore without me, I decided not to take any more of them," she said later. When Joan left Africa a few months later, she, more than any of her fellow volunteers, could hope that what she had done in that village would outlive her presence.

The experience of another volunteer, also a girl working alone in an African village, makes another sharp contrast to the medical project in T. Dianna Paviso is a husky, attractive girl who, in her mid-twenties, went to Senegal in 1964 as an English teacher. No teaching position was waiting for her. Though she had no medical experience, Miss Paviso learned to do simple laboratory analysis and wangled herself a position in a distant provincial hospital. The microscope on which her job depended was delayed, but there was plenty else for her to do. Garbage littered the hospital grounds; the hospital had no running water, although there was piping and a well, because no one had obtained a pump to bring the water from the well to the pipes. Without formal power, Dianna Paviso nonetheless became a force in that small town. She was a familiar figure in the offices of the town's handful of decision makers, politely maneuvering for action on one or another front. She talked the warden of the local jail into lending her prisoners to dig a hole in which to bury the hospital's garbage, and a military friend found a way to obtain a pump for the hospital.

At the hospital, Miss Paviso became acquainted with people from the village of Darsalaam, not far in miles, but totally isolated from even the small modernization available in the town. The village leaders invited her to come "help" Darsalaam, without knowing exactly what they expected of her. Miss Paviso accepted. Two of the village's major health problems were, as usual in Africa, malaria and dysentery caused by impure drinking water. A European drug that controls malaria was available in the town, but its price was very high by village standards and, most important, the drug reduces natural immunity to the disease, so that someone who takes it and then stops is worse off than he was before. However, Miss Paviso discovered that a local bark could be used as a fairly effective malaria suppressant. The bark had in fact been used by the villagers until their conversion to Islam a century ago, but somehow the knowledge had been lost in the change of religious (and therefore medical) authorities. Boiled to make a tea, the bark would help control malaria and provide purer drinking water as well. The difficult part, of course, was convincing the villagers. In her long, slow dialogues with the people of Darsalaam, Dianna Paviso developed strong feelings about how to communicate new ideas in the third world. Her methods, as she later put them down on paper, are a far cry from the canned lectures of the volunteers in the T. project:

They [the villagers] came because they wanted to learn, but very few left any one session having learned what they anticipated. They did not always admit this to me for they wanted me to think that they were learning. The sessions were difficult for them, and they were often frustrated. All their former beliefs about disease were being challenged. . . . Their own language did not have words for the concepts that were being presented to them. [A single word is used for malaria, tuberculosis, and venereal disease.] In the light of this, how could they be expected to change their frame of reference? . . . When they did not understand, they presented questions and offered their own explanations. This was their contribution to me. They were teaching me about their frame of reference — their theory of disease. . . . The villagers had to speak to me first before I was able to speak of anything meaningful to them. . . . More and more it was evident to both the villagers and myself that we were dependent on each other. . . . Not always entirely understanding each other, we were at least joined in a common purpose. . . . The bond that we shared was our one advantage and it made all the difference when times were rough.

Unlike these two girls, most volunteers have been assigned to existing public health operations of one sort or another. Like the rural action volunteers described in Chapter 4, their main purpose is to shore up programs that tend to fall apart at the local level for lack of motivated manpower. In several countries volunteers help to run school lunch programs that use U.S. surplus food.

The Cornell study of Peace Corps impact in Peru concluded that one such school lunch operation showed potential for success. The report stated that the information "indicates that the school pupil feeding program was nearly a perfect program in terms of achieving wide impact in Peru in terms of numbers of clients — children — served, and in terms of local institutions reinforced, assuming that the parents' committees continue to gather strength as volunteer supervisors are withdrawn, and that the Government of Peru can in the long run replace U.S. commodities with local ones. . . ." By 1964 there was reason to be gloomier. The U.S.-provided food was all too often being sold by local officials to line their own pockets. Tragically, many parents, learning that their children were getting food at school, cut back their home feeding to nothing. Volunteers were running away from the program in droves — sometimes, however, after having set up a committee of Peruvians to take their places. However, none of the volunteers gave the nutrition effort the slightest chance to continue once that rapidly dwindling stock of U.S. food surpluses stopped coming from abroad.

A more promising United Nations-sponsored nutrition program was started by the Peace Corps at about this time in another Latin American nation. This one, too, centered on the schools. However, it contained little of the disaster relief implied by U.S. Food for Peace. It was aimed at becoming self-sufficient right from the start. The main giveaway involved was a modest store of garden seeds; with these, volunteers began working at rural schools to establish gardens containing food varieties designed to supplement the dietary deficiencies of the children. At the same time, female volunteers began gaining acceptance for new dishes among teachers and parents, showing them cheap and simple ways of preparing the more nutritious food. One girl's techniques of persuasion were so effective that a group of peasants overcame the most immediate aversion of all — the aversion of the palate. A visitor overheard two peasants arguing: "Must we eat this garbage?" one of them asked in disgust, indicating a vegetable stew. "Yes, the *señorita* says we must set a good example to convince the young ones so they will grow up strong," said the other, and the two closed their eyes and ate.

In other places, volunteers have introduced prepared, low-cost supplements that are high in protein. The surface has only been scratched in such efforts; and here, too, culture calls the tune. Selling these supplements at too low a price has caused people to equate them with animal feed, and even people suffering slow starvation have turned them down.

In 1966-1967, the Peace Corps struck out into a very special field of public health — birth control. This was the result of a general shift in U.S. Government attitudes. Until recently, birth control had been taboo. By 1966, however, the government welcomed the chance to attack the world food crisis by trying to reduce the number of mouths as well as by increasing crop yields. The first big involvement for the Peace Corps came, not surprisingly, in India, the nation where the food-population crisis is most acute.*

India's birth control program, to which the Indian Government had given high priority, used two main methods. For women, it stressed the "loop," a plastic

---

* Like most other agencies involved, the Peace Corps calls what it is doing "family planning," a euphemism which evokes the genteel image of a suburban couple deciding that Dick and Jane are enough.

device inserted in the uterus which prevents pregnancy. The loop is cheap to manufacture (five to ten cents apiece), easily inserted if the woman is in good health, and very easy to remove. For men, the government promoted vasectomy, an operation that blocks the passage of sperm to the penis without interfering with the man's ability to perform the sexual act. The operation is easy and safe if done with minimum competence under sanitary conditions. In theory, vasectomy can be reversed by a second operation, though it is questionable whether this was in fact available to most Indian men.

The first volunteers, who arrived in late 1966, were not expected to insert loops and perform vasectomies. Most were unskilled generalists. A few started in doing extension work, trying to convince Indians to adopt birth control. But most volunteers were working in the program's administration, below the decision-making level. Their main function was to provide the Indian administration with the peculiarly American art of audio-visual aids — slides, movies, picture posters, even puppet shows — all means to extol the virtues of birth control to a largely illiterate audience. In one town, volunteers helped Indians get hold of a sound truck which roamed the streets blaring a recorded announcement: "Get the loop!"

A volunteer couple in the city of Bombay helped bring birth control propaganda to the city's large population of blue-collar workers. They approached plant managers and foremen and worked out a schedule for meetings in the plant where birth control would be explained to the entire work force. The talks to the workers, who do not speak English, were given by Indians.

The volunteers' contribution lay in arranging the meetings, putting up posters, and trying to ensure that everyone showed up on time.

Volunteers attempting to deal directly with Indians about birth control were venturing into particularly deep cultural waters. As we have seen, medicine in general presents cultural dangers for the agent of change, and those dangers are most acute when the agent of change is dealing with the fundamental drive to reproduce. In India, as in any country with high infant mortality, large families are a basic form of security. A Hindu man wants, above most other things in this life, a son to light a candle at his funeral; to be sure one man-child survives to light that candle, the father must produce several babies. Telling him to submit to vasectomy is endangering his security, and removing an essential part of his manhood as well. For an Indian woman, motherhood is the main reason for her existence; depriving her of children deprives her of the work that occupies most of her days.

Some volunteers were worried about the sensitive nature of this work. "The loop isn't toothpaste or insurance," one girl said. "It's something stuck up in the most private portion of a woman." Some were concerned that they, as foreigners, would be particularly vulnerable if there should be popular backlash against birth control. Popular resistance was evident in 1967 in the greatly reduced number of Indians asking for loops or vasectomies; at some clinics, more loops were being removed than inserted. "Many anti family-planning rumors are circulating at the grass roots, quite a few of them true," a former volunteer reported after a tour of rural birth control clinics. The Government of India reacted to the decline in its birth control program in July, 1967, with a desperate-sounding proposal for *compulsory* sterilization of all males with three or more children. (It was later abandoned.) With India in a generally anti-foreign mood that year, many volunteers felt that the popular resentment might fall on them. (The anti-foreign reaction to birth control was not a danger only in India. In Jamaica, a Peace Corps staff member, Ann Anderson, reported seeing a sign that read: BIRTH CONTROL — A PLOT TO KILL BLACK PEOPLE.)

The varied experiences of the Peace Corps have illuminated the many complexities of change in health customs and practices in the third world. The failure of the T. project vividly illustrated the folly of attempting to blitz another culture with American money, technology, manpower and mores. It was doomed from its inception. The isolation from Africa in which the volunteers worked guaranteed their ignorance of reality, but, even had they succeeded in remaking medicine in T. (which they did not), the rest of the country would not have emulated their methods. It cannot afford medical care of such costly proportions.

A more modest and realistic effort, aimed at training low-level public health workers, has been in progress in Ethiopia for four years. The strengths of this program have been that the couple of volunteer doctors involved do not remotely resemble the doctors at T.; and their efforts have been aimed, along with those of volunteer nurses, toward providing skills in Ethiopian workers who, after graduation, work along with traditional healers in curative care, while at the same time making a start on preventive measures in isolated rural areas. The program is far cheaper than the grandiose scheme at T. It takes into account what is feasible in Ethiopia. It is a program largely staffed by Americans, however; as yet the Ethiopian interest has not been strong enough at the ministry level to insure that the work will be taken over eventually by Ethiopians.

At the opposite extreme from the project at T., the individual cases of Joan and Dianna Paviso show that American agents of change in health function best when lack of power and material resources force them to adjust their Western ideas to local realities. In those circumstances, both volunteers were naturally led to offer the people they were among new options in health practices, rather than to try to impose a prefabricated Western system. The case of Joan, who went from troublemaker in the hospital to an outstanding performer in the village, is particularly revealing. Joan's metamorphosis seems to have been due mainly to her escape from the all-American environment of her colleagues and the direction of the doctor volunteers.

The increasing use by the Peace Corps of generalists — by 1967, close to three-fourths of the fourteen hundred volunteers in health assignments were generalists without previous medical training — is a potentially important demonstration to nations that cannot afford the high-priced skills of the medical profession. Its shift from curative medicine to public health is also a move toward more economic use of scarce manpower.

The Peace Corps itself has had considerable difficulty applying what it has learned about public health. The lag is of course common in human affairs; it is one thing to learn that cigarettes cause cancer, another to quit smoking. But the Peace Corps has run into problems that arise from its own, American culture. The agency has not been able to cope with the American medical profession. American doctors are as zealous in protecting the secrets and privileges of their trade as are the traditional healers of the third world; and Peace Corps officials are as reverent as denizens of the third world in their approach to the profession.

Doctors, as a result, receive a deference from the Peace Corps accorded to no other group. No volunteer doctor has ever been dropped by the Peace Corps during his training (except for reasons of health). Overseas, volunteer doctors have received kid-glove treatment. The two doctors who were responsible for much of the trouble in the T. project went home voluntarily, over the staff's efforts to convince them to stay; had they not been doctors, they might well have been sent home earlier, and certainly no one would have tried to induce them to stay. The lessons of the T. project were not fully absorbed by the agency. Even as the T. project was ending, the staff in a nearby country was launching a similar project, even though that staff knew all about the T. disaster. A year later this new project looked a great deal like T., and the Peace Corps was spending a great many hours trying to decide what to do about the doctors who, once more, were at the root of much of the trouble. In both cases, Peace Corps officials, like most Americans, proved unable to treat doctors like other human beings. The agency has had more problems with its volunteer doctors, considering how few they are (twenty in 1967), than with any other category of volunteers.

Even where it appears to be successful, the effect of the Peace Corps health work cannot be measured like crop yields or percentages of students passing an examination. It is tempting, nonetheless, to speculate on the long-run potential of the volunteers' work in providing protein to infants and small children. Lack of protein in early childhood apparently causes lack of mental stamina in adults, and therefore may be in part responsible for the passive acceptance of fate characteristic of the third world. So infant protein could be a revolutionary weapon. Large-scale feeding of protein to infants and children might produce, a generation later, a harvest of men and women dedicated to change and able to grapple successfully with their environment. Today, of course, this is no more than speculation. Like most development issues, the question of motivation is a product of a great number of factors, not answered by anything as simple as eating more protein. Undoubtedly proteins, the basic building blocks of life, are essential to the proper functioning of an organism, whether an individual organism or a whole social body. But what is the best way to provide imprived nutrition? Is it by direct intervention in child feeding? Or is it, under the circumstances of disorganization and difficult communications found in so much of the third world, through some less personal measure such as opening up roads and markets to the hinterland? These questions cannot be answered by any rules of thumb. Public health programming, like planning for agricultural change, must be adapted to a wide variety of local circumstances.

The intangible that may be the surest contribution of the Peace Corps to the third world in health is the quality simply called "caring." The case for this contribution was eloquently stated by Leslie Hanscom, a Peace Corps official, after a 1966 visit to volunteer nurses in a remote Asian country. Hanscom wrote:

To meet them in the street, these people are as uncomely a lot as God ever made. Every outrage that smallpox, trachoma, tuberculosis, malnutrition and miscellaneous infection can work on the human frame is advertised in their appearance. The all-white eyeball and the face pockmarked to the texture of a sea sponge are sights that contribute to the outlander's first culture shock.

Not many Westerners would relate to them at first sight. They are too exotic in their garb and manners. . . . The common man tends to be highly scented with essence of goat. To offset this, the men walk around with lilacs and roses, which makes them appear all the more strange. When you see a typical citizen answering nature's call by squatting over the open ditch system from which people dip their water, it doesn't help to note that he is holding a rose in his teeth.

Fellow feeling for them doesn't come in a rush. The place to be smitten with the truth that these are sharers in the common bloodstream of humanity is in an Asian hospital. Here the human basics come to the fore and blot out oddities of culture. The flies that swarm around the stains on the bed linen may be a novel sight, but the spectacle of pain is all too familiar. The father who has slept for weeks on the floor by the bedside of a small girl with an amputated arm, the child who sleeps under the bed of a mother eaten by cancer are reminders that the family of man is a wide one.

For this reason, I believe the profoundest people-to-people encounter to be witnessed in this nation is what goes on between the sick in Asian hospitals and the Peace Corps nurses. To see them work is to be struck by the power that can be exerted by a little common decency. Moreover, it is not just the visiting outsider who is struck, but the local hospital workers who are there to stay.

There are strong reasons why it has an almost startling effect upon the people to see an American girl in a white uniform appearing to take their troubles to heart. They themselves have been conditioned by life to stifle human sympathy in their own natures. Most of them, by the time they are ten years old, have witnessed more misery and disaster than an American would see in several lifetimes. To cut themselves off from involvement is a way of protecting themselves from an expenditure of feeling that would drain them dry.

They do feel for their own closest kin. Any hospital you visit is filled with heart-touching examples of this. I saw a whole family — mother, father, brothers, sisters — clustered around in an agony of apprehension while a volunteer doctor unwrapped the swaddling bands from a baby suffering from an obstruction of the bowels. But the immediate family unit usually contains such a proliferation of woe that there is no sympathy to spare for outsiders.

The practical instinct to shrink from the suffering of others is fully shared by Asian nurses. Their attitude toward the ill is ironically close to the ancient Oriental attitude toward the leper — "unclean, don't touch." Before the advent of the Peace Corps, there was almost nobody to drum it into them that not turning aside from the spectacle of suffering is what their trade is all about.

From all signs, the lesson is now taking hold. Asian nurses see the patients' surging emotional response to the Peace Corps girls, and — out of plain jealousy — try to divert some of this to themselves. That the response exists is unmistakable. It seems to be true that, of all the services that the Peace Corps can confer, the one that makes the deepest impression on the recipient is ministering to the ailing body.

While the quality of caring may be most graphically demonstrated in hospitals, prisons and orphanages — closed institutions for the dying and unwanted — it also was an essential quality of Joan's and Dianna Paviso's work. Caring is concern and interest: it matters in a community of ordinary people as well as in a closed institution. A volunteer who cares enough to learn will probably make a contribution not only in public health but in other Peace Corps jobs as well.

6

THE PEACE CORPS IN
COMMUNITY DEVELOPMENT

"I believe the core of the Peace Corps mission is to change men's minds, not in their thoughts about America, but in their thoughts about themselves, their surroundings, and their own ability to improve them."

These were the words of a young summer intern working at Peace Corps headquarters as a part of his university degree program. His statement, which summed up his thoughts on the summer's internship, went on: "Furthermore, this idea is not wishful thinking, but the basis of the community development discipline."

The young intern had never served overseas, yet his statement of Peace Corps purpose would find agreement among many Peace Corps veterans. There are others, however — some civil rights workers, campus activists, peace proponents, and even a significant number of Peace Corpsmen — who would see in this state-

ment merely another of the many disguises for the Western paternalists' need to dominate. It is not hard to
imagine that the young intellectual revolutionaries of
the third world, those who are reading Frantz Fanon's
The Wretched of the Earth, would also find repugnant
the idea of Americans changing men's thoughts. They
see Americans as belonging to the world's reactionary
minority, holding their positions of entrenched privilege
by means such as "community development" designed
to narcotize the oppressed multitudes.

The fact is that everyone is trying community development these days: rich, poor, guerrilla revolutionary
and military strongman alike. To speak of a "community
development discipline," however, is to stretch a point.
Even today (much less in 1961) there is no method
that can clearly be defined for intervening in the lives
of the poverty-stricken to change their fundamental orientation. In the decade of the sixties community development methods and ideology vary all the way from
shooting those who don't want change to buying their
compliance with food and other goodies. When Peace
Corps volunteers first went overseas to do community
development they were going into unknown jobs with
only the vaguest commission in hand. Community development, a fuzzy concept first articulated in England
in 1948, had matured hardly at all. A few examples existed — a private program in the Philippines, the village-
level worker effort in India. These, however, had produced inconclusive results or disappointment, or, at
best, small islands of possible success. In those early
days there were only a few people who called themselves
community development experts, and these were largely

erratic (though often charismatic) characters who, despite personal successes, had little method that they could pass on to others.

"Development" was viewed as "progress," and vice versa. When pressed, the more articulate community developers launch into monologues about democracy-in-action. Projects were supposed to satisfy some sort of locally-felt needs, but there were few restraints upon the community developer to keep him from selecting among "felt needs" to emphasize those that best suited his own tastes. Practically any activity could be described as community development. One volunteer pointed out the fancy metal beds newly acquired by the girls of the local bordello, the fruits of their having joined a Peace Corps-assisted savings and loan cooperative. "That," the volunteer proudly asserted, "is community development . . . "

The approach to people could be paternal, almost coercive. In one big city slum volunteers showed movies in a community center built with AID money. The films came from USIS (the United States Information Service) free, but the volunteers were charging admission and holding on to the money for worthwhile community projects. Social behavior at the movies was strictly policed by the volunteers. "We run the operation like a Marine battalion," they said. Were there any local people involved in the project? "We did it without them because they probably would have been corrupt. We don't want them messing up our project!" When asked what they called their Peace Corps assignment, one of them unhesitatingly replied, "Urban community development."

Not all Peace Corps efforts in community development have been so autocratic. In another country, a
volunteer talked the people of his small rural community into reactivating a town council that had been
defunct for more than a decade. As a result of his accomplishment, the volunteer gained a reputation as a community developer. A visiting Peace Corps dignitary
from Washington requested to see the town council in
action. The volunteer agreed and got the council's permission to admit this outsider. The Washington official sat through a long session in which plans were
discussed for levying a voluntary tax to support the
council's general fund. Then the council's president politely requested that the volunteer and his visitor leave
the meeting while an "affair of some importance" was
discussed. Outside, the volunteer explained that the
sensitive matter up for discussion probably had something to do with electing a new town treasurer. "You
see," the volunteer said, "the reason the council went
out of business ten years ago was that the treasurer used
the town's money on his girlfriend. They're probably going to elect the same guy treasurer again." "What!" said
the Washington visitor, "you've got to get back in there
and stop them!" The volunteer patted his visitor's
shoulder. "Don't sweat it, dad — anyhow, my sources
tell me the guy is ready to pay part of the money back."

In a steaming jungle town on the Magdalena River
in Colombia a volunteer talked about the kinds of work
other volunteers in the vicinity were doing. The conver-
sation covered teaching, public health, physical education, a quixotic and financially disastrous venture into
agricultural marketing cooperatives. The volunteer hesi-

tated: "Look," he said, "the real job is community development. When volunteers don't realize that they're in trouble." These were almost exactly the words we had heard a week earlier from an official of the Colombian agency, Acción Comunal. We have heard the same idea from volunteers all the way from Manila to Patagonia. Just to say it, however, does not define it. There is something abstract about the concept that slips through one's fingers, unlike teaching or public health or agriculture, which immediately call to mind busy-sounding jobs associated with concrete objects: schools, clinics, plows. The community development volunteer similarly feels the concept slipping through his fingers when he arrives at his site and surveys what seems to lie ahead of him. He knows very little about the town into which he has just dropped — often he knows nothing at all, and no one is there to meet or welcome him. He has with him a footlocker of books provided by the Peace Corps — a few titles on community development and social change, but most of the books are light entertainment. He knows that his job has no set hours, no fixed office in which to work. He has only his Peace Corps orders, which tell him little more than to go to the town and "develop" it. Such a volunteer is often tempted to spend his time with the books he has brought, meanwhile trying to recall just what they said community development was in training.

In trying to come to grips with this subject, Director Jack Vaughn said: "One-quarter of our volunteers are in community development. And yet, though you hear a number of theories about the job, no one can tell you what community development is!" Vaughn's professed ignorance picked the diplomat's course among conflicting opinions. Almost anyone in the Peace Corps seemed willing to take a crack at a definition of community development. Most definitions told more about the person making them than about how society works. The ease with which people conjured up at least a hunch about community development attested to their belief that change in human affairs is more than a random process.

They sensed that some force could be applied to make the difference between want and sufficiency, between apathy and independence, between war and peace. They hoped to be able to identify the process of change in human affairs so as to be able to serve it — hasten it — with well-planned intervention. This intervention might take the form of materials — fertilizer or educational TV sets. It might be human beings with skills that are needed — a teacher or an engineer. It might be new information relating to productivity or administrative structure — a way of planting rice or making capital available to co-ops. It might be the introduction of new forms of energy other than the sweat of human brows — a donkey or a tractor. Or it might be a combination of all these.

Some communities, it was obvious, were able to act collectively and some were almost totally helpless; some were bursting with determination to solve their problems and others seemed almost devoid of motivation to change. In the one case, the efforts of the community developer seemed hardly needed. In the other, the majority of the third world's communities, some outside stimulus clearly was called for. The trouble was, as the preceding examples illustrate, every community development volunteer picked a different way to go about applying that outside stimulus. Peace Corps programmers threw up their hands and assigned to community development any new recruit who seemed to have no definable skills. Volunteers were sent out to start projects more or less on their own initiative. Their bridges and latrines and drainage ditches were constantly being photographed for inclusion in the Peace Corps reports to Congress as proof that our boys were winning the war against poverty — the "root cause of communism" — Over There. Their assignments were designated as "unstructured" as opposed to the "structured" (i.e., nine-to-five or its local equivalent) jobs of teaching in schools and nursing in hospitals. The distinction still remains today, long after experience has demonstrated that successful work in community development requires a systematic application of some method, which, in turn, tends to create its own kind of structured job.

An example of how far volunteers could wander into the mists of "unstructured" jobs occurred in the early days in Peru. They were given the title "Community Developer" and packed off to the high reaches of the Andes, to the godforsaken deserts of the coast, to the Amazon jungles, to tackle a vast variety of projects, all the way from slum housing to pre-school teaching. For the most part, these projects were left to the volunteer himself to discover. The Peace Corps staff in Peru, dismally small in number, seldom was able to visit the volunteers in their sites or give them adequate supervision. Yet, throughout all of Peru, a strong feeling of purpose pervaded the efforts of the volunteers. That purpose was to stimulate a vast social revolution among the dis-enfranchised and exploited masses of Peruvian Indians by awakening in them a spirit of hope. Volunteers sensed that change would never come to Peru until the Indian insisted on his right to stand up and be counted. The Peace Corps director there, a brilliant man with a deep understanding of the political process, trusted American youth to such an extent that he scarcely questioned the ability of an average volunteer to transmit a feeling of self-reliance to Peruvian Indians.

What happened? At best, 10 percent of the volunteers were creative enough and persistent enough to discover for themselves the way to go about their job.

Another 30 to 50 percent of the volunteers managed to hang onto their projects through thick and thin, enduring the inaction or passing whims of their Peruvian counterparts, plugging away at the given job, be it mixing powdered milk from Wisconsin dairy farms for school lunches or dispensing aspirin at poorly-equipped health posts thirteen thousand feet above sea level. Their accomplishments were usually minor and transitory. Another group, perhaps as much as 30 percent of the volunteers in Peru, wandered almost at will from site to site, project to project, killing time and seeing the country, or bumbling from one failed project to another until their two years' service was up.

An example of the worst of this type, by no means a unique case, was a volunteer who in quick succession: tried to break a pony to harness in order to introduce new motive power to the community (the horse ran away, harness and all, project abandoned); promoted a communal nursery for reforestation and undertook to care for ten thousand seedlings himself (three weeks later he departed on vacation, and, on his return, found all the seedlings dead); pushed the idea of hot showers for the school, promoted materials to construct them and whipped up interest among the unwashed to do the manual labor (after two weeks of effort he tired of the job and abandoned the direction of it, materials and tools and project soon vanishing); encouraged some young men to buy band instruments at great expense to themselves, promising to teach them to play and form a band (abandoned when he found they wanted to play only Indian music, which he didn't like); undertook to mount the community's two-hundred-dollar gasoline sprayer on a horse's back for greater efficiency (the horse, never having heard a gasoline engine before, much less from the proximity of his own back, quickly divested himself of the machine, totally wrecking it); took the community Jeep to pieces with the intent of repairing it but somehow never managed to get the parts back together again.

Certainly that should have been enough. The unfortunate residents of his community were, in addition, visited by yet another disaster: a second volunteer, who offered to castrate a farmer's prize donkey, using what he described as American methods. The donkey bled to death. The farmer's son (who had introduced the volunteer to the family) was held responsible and eventually had to leave the community in shame for the coastal slums.

This list of small disasters gives an idea of what can go wrong with community development. By no means were all Peru volunteers so failure-prone. The research

study on Peace Corps impact in Peru undertaken by
Cornell University concluded that the volunteers had
been of measurable help in strengthening Peruvian institutions. The research was rough and somewhat vague
in defining the indicators of development that were
used as measures, but it was by no means as rough and
vague as the Peace Corps program it was commissioned
to study.

The most organized approach to projects was tried
in the African country of Gabon. The Peace Corps responded to Gabon's request for assistance in school
construction with what we might call Seabee tactics.
Using materials provided by American foreign aid, the
volunteers, under the direction of a retired military man,
hit the beaches of Gabon with trucks and bulldozers.
They slashed their way through the jungles, putting up
schools at a dizzying rate, and moved on with their
heavy equipment to new sites. Occasionally a volunteer
would fraternize with the locals, but it certainly was not
part of his job. Nobody had asked him to see that the
schools were wanted by the communities in which they
were erected, or that they were used after they were put
up. The concerns discussed in Chapter 3, "The Peace
Corps in Teaching," did not disturb the cadres of that
blitz in Gabon. Schools were built. No one could deny
that, and this tangible fact seemed to satisfy them.

In Ecuador the Peace Corps tried another kind of
school construction. Volunteers attempted to see if the
communities wanted schools, and if Ecuadorians would
maintain and staff them after they were built. Local
labor was used to assist the construction, as well as some
local materials. In the end, targets for classroom con-

struction remained woefully unmet, for the project —
the school — was the main goal, and any attempts to
involve the people in a self-help scheme were gestures
which backfired and successfully clogged all the pipe-
lines to the sizable American aid that was involved.* If
nothing but classrooms were the goal, the Gabon Seabee technique was clearly superior.

Such projects dominated the agency's publicity in
the early days, and were often described as community
development. Another approach was also being tried. In
this approach, the projects were not considered as ends
in themselves but as means to an end, exactly what end
often proving elusive. Generally the end was expressed
in terms of "self-help" — helping people learn to solve
their own problems with the resources at hand. The
oldest and best example was in Colombia, where several
hundred volunteers, calling themselves without apology
community development workers, were assigned to the
Colombian agency, Acción Comunal. This agency
shared the self-help view of community development
that was being inculcated in volunteers by the Peace
Corps. It had a staff of trained workers with whom volunteers were frequently paired, and it covered most of
the country. Without Peace Corps help, Acción Comunal might have disappeared in 1962, when it was still
shaky, insecure and overextended.

A typical site was Blanquita, in the coffee-growing
highlands of Colombia, a town of one thousand people
located some forty miles from its departmental capital.

* This case is reminiscent of the school-to-school fiasco described
in Chapter 4 — a "project" effort that did not even result in a project,
let alone any other gain.

Surrounding Blanquita are thirty *veredas*, hillside rural neighborhoods, each with its own name and sense of identity. A community development volunteer, Tony, put in two years in Blanquita. His method of operation was to talk with the citizens informally until he began to sense a common need for some kind of modest community project. Tony then began to cultivate the community leaders, talking to them about the need to form an action committee to get the town moving. With the help of his Colombian counterpart, an employee of Acción Comunal, he convened a meeting of the citizens, who then elected a slate of officers. The committee then tackled some simple action projects, things that could be finished quickly and satisfied some need felt by the townsmen. Having repaired the front entrance to the church, organized a fiesta in honor of Blanquita's patron saint, and painted the police station (all with local resources), the committee felt it was ready to take on something more arduous. They looked to Tony for advice.

What finally resulted in Blanquita was a mile of water pipe which, for the first time in history, brought water to the center of the town. The pipe was secured partly through money raised in town and partly through a donation from the powerful Federation of Coffee Growers. It was installed by the villagers themselves. No longer did the women have to walk the mile uphill to the spring with their five-gallon kerosene cans on their backs. When Tony's two-year tour of duty was up, Blanquita was closed as a Peace Corps site. The job had been done. The town was on its own, the committee confident and active.

If the story of Blanquita had been left at the day of Tony's departure, a day redolent of amity and tears, there would have been nothing but glory in it for all parties concerned. A year and a half later, however, a visit to Blanquita disclosed that water no longer ran out of the pipe in the center of town. Inspection showed that the intake was clogged. On further investigation it was found that the citizens of the town had become divided against each other, the action committee inactive. What had happened?

A farmer up on the hillside, living in one of the *veredas* along the pipeline but not part of the Blanquita community, had turned on his spigot to irrigate his small banana plantation. As a result, only a dribble of water was left in the pipe by the time it reached town. When the committee sent delegates up to the farmer to instruct him to stop irrigating with the town's domestic water supply, the farmer told them to go soak their heads in the spring. No legal provision had been made to safeguard the water supply of Blanquita. Nothing could be done. Eventually the source plugged up for lack of maintenance and the farmer, no mechanic, was unable to get enough water for even his own household. Back to the kerosene cans.

Several significant mistakes, mostly of omission, were made in Blanquita. One had to do with the nature of a community. Tony assumed that the community included only the town of Blanquita. Though he had worked extensively in the *veredas* around the town as well, he considered them all separate communities, each to be treated as distinct. He did not consider that the farmer's *vereda* was integral to the well-being of

Blanquita in the matter of the water pipe. To carry it further, he did not include the whole political subdivision in which Blanquita was located, and from which it derived its legal powers, as a part of the community with which he had to deal in this affair. Indeed, all of the nation was to some extent involved.

Tony and his Colombian counterpart also assumed that forming a new organization, the action committee, was good of itself. In actuality, the seeds of increased conflict were sown the minute new leaders threatened the old in Blanquita. Old factionalisms were stirred which only burst into flame after Tony had departed, when the farmer intercepted the prize water supply. Creating a new organization in town escalated conflict to the point of breakdown. Organizing a new committee was not the only way open to Tony for supporting local leadership. He might have worked through the existing leaders.

An example from another country illustrates the same point. A rural community development volunteer formed an action committee to get his project done. An existing committee that had been dormant suddenly came to life as a result of the threat from the upstarts. The old committee took over the project, finished it successfully, and caused the total collapse of the volunteer-supported committee.

In both cases the volunteers were ignorant of existing social structure. Co-ops, as another instance, have been tried by volunteers all over the third world with a notably high failure rate. In one case in the Andes, however, volunteers found they could succeed by using the existing social framework. The Indians were too suspicious to join foreign-designed cooperatives of the usual kind. Changing their tactics, the volunteers were able to organize effective small co-ops based on the family, already a viable economic unit. These family-based cooperatives rapidly produced a measurable gain in income, according to the volunteers.

Finally, Tony assumed that he had done his community research when he had begun to identify the wants of the people — the "felt needs," in the language of community development. They felt they needed repairs to the front door of the church; they felt they needed a fiesta for their patron saint and paint for the police station. A pipeline, the people of Blanquita realized in due course, was a need. Another very real need, however, was for legal protection of the water supply, and for the cooperation of the *vereda* residents whose land was crossed by the pipe. This need Tony did not comprehend. He had not done all his research.

Blanquita illustrates the fine line between success and failure in community development. In all honesty, no one can say whether the cause of development was served there. It may be that in several more years the leadership developed by Acción Comunal and the Peace Corps in the case of the pipeline will come to the fore again. It may be that the demonstrated benefits of self-help and cooperation will someday cause the citizens to rally behind another project and forget their divisions. These are the unmeasurables. All one can state now is that community development in Blanquita was not as successful as it might have been.

A recent self-help program in the United States provides an analogy. Northern youths went to Mississippi

to register Negro voters. The purpose was to develop a
spirit of self-reliance in Southern Negroes by helping
them to become a part of the political process. As a direct consequence, black men lost their jobs in Mississippi or were thrown off their sharecropper's holdings.
People were beaten. Some were shot. A Negro political
party was formed and duly rejected by the ruling white
majority and some middle-class Negroes. Black power, a
concept not in the dreams of the Northern youths who
originally went to Mississippi, hung in the sultry Delta
air like the forewarning of a tornado. The Mississippi
story, like that of Blanquita, suggests exciting possibilities. But there is also something risky and half-cocked
about an outsider going into a community to get something — anything — started   and   then   abandoning
the people. Defeat in either Blanquita or Mississippi
may simply plunge the people into a deeper apathy, convincing them that the idea of progress was only a dream
after all, just as the cynics said from the beginning.

Community development in the Peace Corps took a
step forward when it began to favor self-help programs
over random projects. The project approach all too frequently assumed that an "improvement" which looked
good to the volunteer, a foreigner, would also look good
to the person whose life was supposed to be changed
by it. Self-help at least tried to take into account the
needs of the client population, its desires, and its own
budding awareness of its problems. The step forward
was a small one, however, especially in those cases
where self-help was promoted by the Peace Corps in
places where the local resources to effect improvements
did not exist.

More recently, some of the volunteers in the field, some of the people in the United States who were training volunteers, and a few Peace Corps staff members, had begun to look at community development from a different point of view. They saw it as a *process*, a dynamic in human affairs, by which people meet the challenges of their environment. A project, let us say a new community center, is just a building; behind that building stretches out in time the complex process by which the people of the community decided they wanted that building and went about getting it. The community development worker is someone who has attempted to understand this process and who then intervenes where his efforts will do the most good to set the process in motion, or to speed it up, eventually to make it produce the kind of change that will result in economic, social and political development.

A case from the early years of the Peace Corps illustrates how an outsider, a volunteer, can intervene fundamentally in the lives of people with a minimum of his own cultural bias showing. In 1962 Ralph Bolton, recently graduated from college in international relations, arrived as a volunteer in Peru. His first work, a temporary job, took him out among Quechua-speaking Indians near Puno, on the shores of Lake Titicaca, where there are some of the greatest population densities on earth. His assignment was to interview the Indians and collect information about their social and economic relationships — a vague social science project of the local university. In the summer of 1963, disastrous flooding destroyed the land and property of hundreds of Indian families in this region. The Puno Development Corporation, a Peruvian organization, hastily commissioned Bolton to use his information about these Indians to help develop a relocation plan for them. What resulted was a self-governing cooperative colony for seventy families.

The colony was located fifty miles away from the shores of the lake on land purchased from a large land-owner with a long-term loan. Bolton in 1964 was living in a temporary sod hut on a hillside with the other colonists above the spot where they were constructing more permanent buildings. Fields were being laid out and plowed, irrigation works being planned, and herds of llamas and alpacas grazing the high flanks of the hills. The women had already started carding and spinning alpaca wool for market. This eventually led to an industry producing jackets for market in the United States, as well as other handicraft articles (such as simple tapestries done by the children of the colony depicting local scenes with great expressiveness). A school had been established, producers' and consumers' cooperatives begun, herds pooled to upgrade breeding, and continuing sources of development capital and technical advice arranged. Bolton described his role as that of expediter, putting together technology and capital from Peruvian and other sources, and idea man. He scrupulously avoided interfering in the self-governing apparatus of the colonists, but at the same time kept himself on tap in case they wanted his suggestions.

The new colony would never have become a reality without Bolton. His success in this venture stemmed largely from his systematic study of the people he intended to work with. He lived among the Indians and shared their life, and he made a diligent effort to learn their language, Quechua. In short, he did not act until he had acquired some understanding of the process of change; thus he was able to anticipate some of the problems involved in the precedent-shattering move of the seventy families. Bolton's knowledge of the people gave him the assurance he needed to help create a new community out of many diverse elements. His goal was, in his words, to make "an experiment in agrarian reform . . . not one of those long-range, high-cost programs for a whole nation, but a demonstration that could be done relatively cheap and fast." Referring to the incredible misery and injustice under which the Peruvian Indian lives, he said: "It's got to be relatively fast and cheap. The time is short."

Bolton had, in addition to his other strengths as a community development worker, extraordinary patience, a quality which helped him to work with technicians, upper-class figures, and the mestizos of the region — all of whom tend to look down on the Indian. Because no qualified volunteer was available to continue the work at the colony, and because the whole experiment remained shaky, Bolton decided to extend his service by one more year, through 1965. Since his departure, the colony has continued to have problems. A recent observer who knows the colony said, "It is a village of seventy families still living in misery, still undernourished, still in poverty." The experiment has tied up seventy thousand dollars in long-term loans and cost another thirty thousand dollars in current expenses which have not been met by income. Management has always been a critical problem, with planning often done on a day-to-day basis and with little recognition given to the complexity of establishing a working cooperative. Most distressing for the community developer interested in the developmental process, the attitudes of the Indians toward their environment appear to have changed only slightly, making the colony little different from communities nearby. The introduction of a school and new technology have not changed the way the people live. Infant mortality has not declined. It was Bolton's contention that giving the people a measure of autonomy would produce, in time, the changes in attitudes needed to make the experiment work. At the present, the question is whether the experiment can survive long enough for these changes to take place. As a volunteer in Costa Rica, Ralph Harbison, pointed out, no one knows how long it takes for attitude changes to "surface" in a person's outward behavior. Yet Bolton's effort must be counted a bold experiment under far from ideal conditions. The families who originally decided to make the move to the new colony were not selected for their desire to innovate, but rather for their need. Management was far from adequate. Peruvian society remains dominated by a sleepy class of oligarchs who are not about to invest, at the rate of one hundred thousand dollars per seventy families, in the future of Peru's millions of destitute Indians. Despite these obstacles, Bolton's experiment at last report was still surviving.

The successful Peace Corps efforts in community development that we have cited have all taken place in rural areas. The urban setting has almost always frustrated the volunteers' best efforts. Urban community development methods have typically been focused on projects: community centers, sewers, credit unions, knitting clubs, day care centers for the children of working mothers. Since 1961 urban community development volunteers have pecked away at such projects, working a few hours a day, fighting the slums' dehumanizing environment and their own depression, with a kind of Christian piety that is as ineffectual as it is admirable. To the volunteers' serial failures the Peace Corps usually reacted with the peculiar expedient of putting new groups back into the same circumstances in which the old had failed. However, in the last two years the Peace Corps has begun to talk about withdrawing from the urban slums. As of this writing, a Peace Corps group that took a leap into the vast slums of Bombay, India, appears to be finishing up without any replacement. In Latin America, the urban contingents have been shrinking.

Where efforts were made to break away from the "project" approach to urban community development and get some kind of self-help program started, there were a few isolated and short-lived successes; material resources, however, are so scarce in the big-city slums that volunteers frequently gave up in despair. The few volunteers who tried to cast themselves in the role of agitator soon discovered that they could not themselves be leaders of the slum communities and generally lacked the common experience and communications skills to stir up potential local leaders. In fact, what the Peace Corps was discovering over the years of bitter discouragement was that the rural and urban settings are quite different. In the vast slums of Lima, Bombay or Lagos, people live in a misery that seems more hopeless than the poverty of the countryside. The social fabric of their lives has been ripped to shreds, and there is seldom a deep sense of identification with a community: they are masses of lost or forgotten individuals. In those overcrowded shantytowns, there do not appear to be any productive resources to which they might turn their idle hands. Uprooted, without opportunity, the slum dwellers are sunk in apathy and despair, imprisoned in their belief that they are helpless.

The Peace Corps volunteer in an urban slum has found his options similarly restricted. He often saw the first need of the people to be the acquisition of some sense of community. Yet he was often stuck with a project which produced little, if any, hope in the people involved. Often he was paired with, or placed under the supervision of, a social worker. He then found himself identified with that profession and had to break down the well-justified suspicion which many social workers arouse as a result of their obvious distaste for the lower classes. In one Latin American city a volunteer reported that a slum dweller lit a cigarette in the presence of just such an official. "Did I give you permission to smoke?" the official demanded sharply, sounding like those urban volunteers, described at the beginning of this chapter, who ran their movie operation like a Marine battalion.

Peace Corps programmers came to feel that the rural volunteer worked in a setting with greater potential (although by the standards of American opulence there is little apparent difference between city starvation and rural famine). The people with whom a rural volunteer works have a sense of community — a permanence not to be found in the big city, where the average period of residence in a neighborhood may be as short as six months. In the country, family and other institutions remain strong points of reference, no matter how desperate the conditions. Villagers, though on the fringes of a money economy, at least have the activity of subsistence farming; they are not rotting in unemployment like the people of the slums. A volunteer often could find more productive resources with which to work in the countryside, and he could focus his efforts on one or several distinct communities, rather than on a vast, shifting slum. And, of course, the urban-rural contrast existed in the volunteers' own society. Americans could point with pride to the rapid development of their own rural sector. To their own big-city slums, however, they could only refer with shame.

In the last few years, two new approaches to directed change have come to the attention of the Peace Corps, one related to rural programs and the other to urban. In 1964 and 1965 a group of men from Michigan State University's Institute for Community Development began to train volunteers for work in rural Chile in what they called a "holistic approach" to community development. The holists held that if some "model" (i.e., a simplified version of a complex reality) could be designed which would explain human behavior in terms that an agent of change could grasp, then he would be able to see ways in which he could influence that behavior. The Michigan State men — Iwao Ishino, Edmond Alchin, John Donoghue and Stewart Marquis — advanced a model and tried it out. In their behavior model, "images" (the communications term meaning the way a person views the world) determine a person's plans for using the resources at his command. His plans then determine what action he will take with those resources. Finally, his evaluative mechanism, that introspective faculty which distinguishes man from the beasts and makes him look inward, causes him to appraise the results of his action and, if necessary, change his images and then his planning, and so on. The process might be illustrated by the stonecutter who picks up a tool, takes a couple of whacks with it, examines the stone and is dissatisfied, puts the tool down, rummages around for what he now feels will be a better tool, and then tries again. Probably all of us can remember times when new information or new ideas have caused us to see the world differently, and therefore to act in new ways. As a personal example particularly pertinent to community development, we recall our first reading of Saul Alinsky, the radical organizer of the urban poor in the United States. After that, we were unable to look at urban ghettoes without seeing the powerlessness described by Alinsky. Our images of ghettoes, and therefore our behavior, had changed in response to the new images, although of course the ghettoes themselves had not changed.

The task of the community development worker is to find ways of changing people's images (often inaccurately called "changing attitudes") so that their plans and actions will change. In order to do so he must know a great deal about people's images, and how their plans are affected by their images. He must also know a great deal about the resources upon which people's plans hinge. New plans, after all, are useless without the resources — money, skills, or whatever — needed to carry

them out. To discover this information the volunteer must undertake operational research, taking care not to let his own values, or images, usurp the field and warp his study by dictating what people would be thinking if they were he rather than what they actually do think.*
He must, for example, see what people see when they look at him — not the quite different image he sees when he looks in his mirror. In what must by now be a tremendous number of cases all over the world, volunteers have found doors gradually opening to them in their communities when, after a probation period of one to six months, the people decided the volunteers were not CIA agents, or some other kind of threat, as had been rumored. Volunteers, however, frequently do not realize exactly what is holding up their acceptance; they only begin to find out after images have changed and someone in the village says, "For a long time we thought you were a spy. . . ."

In the last three years Peace Corps volunteers have shown that they can be trained in the field research techniques necessary to compile the information they need. Using a systematic method of community study, the volunteer came to understand which members of a community were influential in which activities. He discovered that each of the many systems operating in the community had its own characteristic set of images, its

---

* Dianna Paviso, the volunteer in public health quoted in Chapter 5, understood this point ("The villagers had to speak to me first before I was able to speak of anything meaningful to them. . . ."). The Michigan State men likewise stress that the operational research required by the holistic approach is not an academic exercise. It cannot be done from an ivory tower. It requires continuous personal involvement, as well as an ability to deal effectively with emotions and values, including the researcher's own.

view of what was reality, and its own in-group. The kin-ship system had its own codes of behavior and influential people, as did the political system, the religious, the economic and the voluntary associations. The influence of these central figures was interrelated, overlapping and tied together by links of communication. The volunteer trained in the holistic approach tried systematically to understand communication links through his research; and when the real problems of the community began to appear out of his study of images, he acquired a more sure knowledge of where to apply his energies, what projects were possible, and where self-help would work. If Tony had done this kind of homework in Blanquita, his pipeline might have continued to carry water.

Two groups of volunteers trained in the holistic approach were sent to Chile in 1964 and 1965. Another was sent to Colombia in 1966 as the first major change from the type of community development that was practiced in Blanquita. The volunteers in these ground-breaking ventures have not been used as effectively as they might have been. Even so, they have shown a significantly greater ability than previous volunteers to understand their overseas environment and to come to grips with the problems of the people with whom they have been assigned. One such volunteer in his first year overseas was able to gain support and acceptance in a community of miners that is 85 percent Communist. In particularly difficult circumstances (the town is dominated by a single mining company) he was able to establish or revive a host of community services, from an ambulance to an infant care center to sports clubs to drainage ditches. The volunteer managed all this by finding ways to open new links between the miners and the company. He became the carrier of new information to all groups in town about what they could accomplish cooperatively. He knew where to feed in the information because he understood the dynamics of the town.

Criticism in the Peace Corps of the holistic method has centered around the fact that applying it is an extremely complex undertaking. The staff feared that volunteers would lack the maturity to push beyond the research stage into action. Such pessimism was, indeed, partly justified. It was based on a growing awareness of the limited maturity and skill of the typical recruit. In several countries, programmers were beginning to come to grips with the complexity of rural development. Given the potential of the average volunteer, they were suggesting that the community development job be broken up into several semi-professional tasks that less-skilled workers could accomplish. Such a set of assignments could be coordinated into a team directed by a more skilled professional, perhaps a volunteer, whose job would be research and planning. In the field, other old hands met these ambitions with skepticism. They had already had experience trying to get volunteers to work together. Volunteers, they said, each want their own area of responsibility: their own culture has conditioned them to go out and "save" someone — a job they regard as personal and not to be shared in any team. They were, perhaps, misreading the evidence. The urge of volunteers to be personally involved in what they are doing has often helped to keep them in close touch with the people they are dealing with, rather than manipulating them from afar. Ralph Bolton, in setting up the colony of transplanted Indians, displayed an ability to work as a member of a team with other volunteers and Peruvians. Without having been trained in it, he was using the techniques of the holistic approach.

Urban community development did not seem so favorable a target for the holistic practitioners. Their heavy emphasis on the use of material resources had less meaning in the slums, where the main resource is human. However, a spate of new ideas on how to work in the slums began to germinate in the United States and abroad just as the Peace Corps was becoming despondent about its own failures. Some of these ideas were the inspiration for an innovation that had nothing to do with the Peace Corps, a private voluntary movement in the Puerto Rican slums. This program, calling itself VESPRA,* began operation in 1965, and by 1967 had become a significant force in the lives of Puerto Rico's poor — the people who inhabit the world of Oscar Lewis's La Vida. VESPRA is determinedly "indigenous," meaning that it is composed of volunteers from the slum communities who continue to live and work where they have always lived. They are street kids, school dropouts; some of them have been in trouble with the law, some are former drug addicts. Almost without exception they are highly motivated to do something with their lives — not necessarily acceptable to the dominant middle class, but something relevant to the slums. VESPRA gives these young men and women the tools to strike directly at the base of the poverty culture: the apathy, helplessness and despair which confound the best

* Voluntarios en Servicio a Puerto Rico Asociados.

efforts of more traditional anti-poverty programs to reach into the hard core of the slums and make dramatic changes.

The tools themselves — group dynamics techniques — are nothing new or revolutionary. VESPRA started with methods developed by an anti-drug addiction program in San Juan. It was demonstrated that a high cure rate could be attained by involving the addicts themselves in making the decisions needed to eliminate dependency on drugs and to find a useful place in society. The methods consisted of getting addicts to examine their attitudes about their environment and themselves and providing group training to give them the confidence and motivation to make new decisions about their way of life, all within the slum community. The founders of VESPRA felt that the same general approach could be used with young adults from the slums to confront social rather than personal hangups. Efrén Ramirez, the psychiatrist who pioneered the drug addiction program, called the technique "attitudinal confrontation training"; others have called it "democratic leadership training" or "motivational training." VESPRA provides its volunteers, who are all essentially healthy people, with training in motivational work with small groups of their peers. It then sends them back into their home communities, slums, and supervises their work with small groups made up of other street people like themselves, people with whom they have grown up. New volunteers are not recruited, in the fashion of the Peace Corps or its domestic equivalent, VISTA. They are selected from among those street people who have shown, by their performance in small groups organized by

VESPRA volunteers, strong motivation and ability to surmount their hangups. These groups are intended to demonstrate the usefulness of group cooperation toward common ends.

VESPRA aimed its original program at the one hundred thousand Puerto Rican youths who are out of school and unemployed. In short order it discovered that it was able to reach people imprisoned in the culture of poverty on the island. Small groups were stepping out into their slums and providing the stimulus for neighborhood organization. Each VESPRA volunteer, through the four or five groups he had formed, was reaching a vastly magnified number of people through the voluntary efforts of the slum people themselves. VESPRA itself is almost invisible: the volunteers are not exotics (like, say, a blond Peace Corpsman in an African village) but slum neighborhood residents who are different only in that they have changed their attitude toward themselves. The people with whom they work are no different from what they always were — except that they attend neighborhood meetings, launch garbage campaigns and painting projects, concern themselves with personal security in the slums, and talk more knowingly about the situation of the poor in Puerto Rican society. They are haltingly, slowly, helping their neighborhoods to acquire a voice. Already the Puerto Rican establishment has heard the new voice of the slum dwellers. A number of communities in the island have said, "We have been forgotten; we demand justice." VESPRA volunteers have been working quietly in these communities, armed with nothing more than their training in group motivation and their conviction that man is responsible for himself — that even in the worst of slums the poor have the right and the responsibility to make the decisions that govern their lives.

When the Peace Corps first heard of the VESPRA experiment it had trouble seeing how all this applied to its own operations. Some in the agency, however, have begun to ask if perhaps Peace Corps volunteers might not be able to establish and support VESPRA-style operations in the big-city slums of Latin America — indigenous, voluntary service programs in which the Peace Corps man would only be an organizer and expediter, not a slum worker himself. In the summer of 1967 the Peace Corps decided to try the idea in Panama, using a few volunteers to support local agents of change.

Out of the Peace Corps experience in community development one constant seems to emerge. To be successful the volunteer has found he has to work with groups rather than just individuals. Ralph Bolton proceeded that way with his agrarian reform colony in Peru. Even Tony, with his marred community development in Blanquita, invested his efforts in support of groups. From farther beyond the Peace Corps sphere comes support for the idea of making groups the basic unit of directed change: from Gandhi, from community development in Yugoslavia, from Albert Camus, from the Italian seer and activist, Danilo Dolci — even from right-wing groups in the United States. From hints about the Vietcong in reports from the Australian Communist Wilfred Burchett, and from a study of the same subject published by M.I.T. Press (*Vietcong*, by Douglas Pike), one senses a considerable application of group methods for community development. Local groups of people with like preoccupations and a common fate seem to be one key to solving society's problems.

A profile of the volunteer who can work with such groups in community development seems to be emerging from the Peace Corps experience. He is probably a generalist, or if he has specialized in his education, his curiosity runs far beyond the confines of his specialty. He is the kind of person who needs relationships with others — who has a compulsion to go out and talk to people rather than remain alone in his room reading his footlocker of books. He most probably is not the kind of person who, in the absence of other leadership, will take action by himself or jump into a leadership role, for, if he did, he would cancel out his goal of stimulating local leadership.

More subtle personality traits may help him to succeed in the complex undertakings we have described here. If one views community development as a series of projects leading in sequence to the development of a poor village, it is simple enough to conceive of one project, say latrines, causing improved health, which in turn leads to more vigor, greater productivity, and thence to a more bountiful and democratic way of life. But if one tries to understand the *process* by which a community develops he must alter his habit of thought radically. The project approach relies on linear (that is, sequential) habits of thought which, Marshall McLuhan assures us, are an inheritance of our long tradition of literacy: thoughts are admitted only one at a time, strung out like words on a page or the innings of a baseball game. The understanding of a process, on the other hand, requires an ability to think about a great number of factors at once. If some of the factors are technological, and some emotional, the complexity is increased. One must be able to grasp the process in its entirety and still find a place to jump in. A lot of things are going on at once in a community. The atmosphere is value-ridden and emotionally charged. "Reality" is not what the volunteer sees, but what the people themselves see and how they feel about it. Human beings are forever in a state of becoming, rather than being. Conflict is always present, and the risk of increased conflict must be accepted (and calculated) when change is introduced deliberately. A community development worker must be able to operate in a preliterate society with its sea of voices breaking against the shores of his own literate rationality. Many authorities in the Peace Corps have said that it is impossible for a volunteer to operate in such a capacity.

Marshall McLuhan offers an interesting observation. The first generation of the electronic age, those under the age of thirty (which includes the vast majority of volunteers), have grown up in an environment in which television surrounds them with a constant flow of images. They have been required to do their homework with the world constantly ebbing and flowing around them. They are conditioned to thinking in terms of process, and to acting when the need arises without waiting for an appropriate full stop which might indicate a clear beginning or end of something. In contrast to the preceding generation, they may be more capable of operating in a preliterate society. This observation may help explain the ability of some volunteers to understand the subtle nature of development, when their elders, the Peace Corps programmers, find difficulty grasping it. It is this complexity that characterizes the process-centered approach used by VESPRA and the holists. The same kind of complexity seems to be involved in most work with groups.

Community development that deals with processes may work, as a Peace Corps job, in only a limited number of countries. Obviously, the ideal place is in a nation where the elite, or at least a dominant faction of the elite, really wants to awaken the masses. Such nations in the third world are few. There are other countries in which confused expressions of interest in the grass roots, plus a certain amount of permissiveness, are to be found in the elite. In such nations, which account for many of the Peace Corps hosts, community development by volunteers has had an equivocal record: successful in some, given the right circumstances and the right volunteers (such as in Brazil, Costa Rica, Niger) and failure in others (India, Iran). There are other countries where dictatorship makes the essentially democratic goal of Peace Corps community development impossible. One exception is Nepal, where an absolute monarch has, for the time being at least, decided that the people will have local self-government at the lowest level. But for the most part this latter group of nations remains impermeable to Peace Corps community development.

Agents trying to motivate people — sometimes outsiders, more frequently not — continue to play a role in the twentieth century revolutions aimed at improving conditions for the hungry masses. Peace Corps community development has often tried to find that role for itself. Many volunteers in different parts of the world have expressed their feeling that their community development work was a substitute for, and in many instances a corrective to, traditional American foreign aid of the plain-dollar variety. Though they usually admit that American dollars and commodities can be useful, and, with good management, can be administered in the third world in nonaddictive doses, they nonetheless see the real need as having to do with the motivation of the masses. It is on this side of the revolution that they see themselves.

It is quite possible that Peace Corps failures in community development have been just as widespread as the failures of more traditional American foreign aid about which taxpayers are so understandably concerned. There are plenty of stumbling blocks in the path of each, in the third world. In some countries, volunteers' efforts to apply their own answer have been confounded by an American ambassador who runs around urging them to take small dollops of money and stick them into "worthwhile" community projects. The ambassador usually calls these "self-help" projects and makes much of them in dispatches to Washington. In one African country the ambassador cornered a bunch of newly arrived volunteers, urging them to come to him for "self-help" funds. (When, later, some volunteers came to him for money to get a latrine-building project under way, the ambassador suggested that some more decorous memorial be chosen.) In defending his use of funds, the ambassador said, "These projects enhance the prestige and influence of the volunteer or technician involved and

thus assure a stronger United States identification."
Usually, volunteers are little interested in buying prestige or influence in their community. However, even if
they were, it would be just about the only return on
the money. Most such "self-help" projects fall into disuse, or get bungled in the execution. What is worse, when
a volunteer gives things away he saddles succeeding
generations of volunteers with the local people's expectations that they will arrive with their own gifts. This
downgrades whatever else they have to offer.

To succeed in community development, volunteers
have had to overcome obstacles more formidable than
ambassadorial largesse. In one Latin American republic
not noted for its determination to humanize the lot of
its peasants, a volunteer put in two years among Indians
living as serfs on a large plantation. As a result of the
volunteer's work the Indians began organizing themselves. The volunteer then began feeding them information about their rights under a new but unheeded
agrarian reform law. Very shortly pained and well-orches-
trated shrieks were heard from the local feudalists. The
government, faced with demands for the volunteer's
expulsion, vacillated for a while, knowing that its
actions were in the public eye. Then it bravely decided
to back the Indians' claim for land — a decision that
more often goes the other way.

In another country, a volunteer befriended a peasant
who had had the temerity to involve himself in a dispute
with the local big landowner. This volunteer, doing
community development in a rural area without roads,
relied on a saddle horse for transportation to the outly-
ing villages. One day the local police impounded his

horse without offering any explanation. It was the oligarchy's way of communicating its displeasure: simple, direct, unmistakably clear. Few community development volunteers would want to let themselves be drawn into such a confrontation. Most would rather get on with the job, which has to do with helping the peasants prepare for that day when there will be no paternal landowner to order their existence.

7

TRAINING: THE EDUCATIONAL
CHALLENGE AT HOME

"If the Edsel Division [of the Ford Motor Company] had been a new department in a university, it would still be there," Arthur Stinchcombe of Johns Hopkins once commented. When the Edsel car failed to sell, Ford discontinued it, while the university, less attuned to the market for its product, may continue a pointless enterprise indefinitely. This innate conservatism of the academic system has posed a major problem to the Peace Corps in the agency's efforts to train volunteers for service overseas.

The Peace Corps decided in 1961 that volunteers should get some form of training before embarking on their missions abroad. At first, training lasted eight weeks; by 1967, it had been lengthened to thirteen weeks or more. Rather than depend on its own training centers — a "Peace Corps Academy" on the lines of West Point was one idea — the agency decided to contract the work out to American colleges and universities. This decision, one of the most important in the brief Peace Corps history, had several bases. Contracting out the training would obviously lessen the work load in those frantic days when the Peace Corps was scrambling to set itself up. Some saw the splendid but rather vague vision of a "partnership" between higher education and the Peace Corps. Sargent Shriver's keen sense of politics also played a part. Shriver was ever anxious to involve the private sector in order to broaden support for his new organization. Here was an opportunity to win over the academic community. University officials and faculty would be involved through the training itself, and plunking the operation down on campus might stimulate more students to join the Peace Corps. From the beginning, therefore, the agency spread its contracts all over the map of the United States, rather than concentrate on a few institutions. Earliest Peace Corps policy unequivocally declared that the new agency would seek a partnership arrangement with the private sector, with emphasis on giving it preference where possible. This policy was to apply both to training and to overseas administration of projects. Most universities were happy enough to get a Peace Corps contract. Though such work did not compare with doing research for the defense establishment as a source of income, the Peace Corps did use the campus in summer, when both buildings and faculty were underemployed; and many academic officials saw no harm in opening new lines of communication to the federal government. By 1968, the Peace Corps had contracted with more than one hundred colleges and universities. A few institutions did training on a year-round basis, but most contracts were for one-shot summer programs.

Though no "Peace Corps Academy" materialized, the agency did set up its own training centers, first in Puerto Rico, which started as a kind of protracted obstacle course for toughening bodies and minds, then in the Virgin Islands. But "in-house" training, as this was called, played only a small part in the early years. Often the question of quality was completely obscured by the administrative chaos in which these centers always seemed bogged. In any event, the great majority of trainees went to the college campus, with only a few experimental projects by industry, labor unions, etc.

The early training programs contained eight basic parts: language, job training, "area" studies (study of the nation to which the trainees were going), American studies, world affairs (i.e., communism), health training, and Peace Corps orientation. It was also a period of selection. Halfway through and again at the end, trainees considered unfit to go overseas for one reason or another were dropped. The trainees were tested in various ways, almost always under observation by the many psychologists on the staff.

Those early campus-bound training operations were grim. A visit to the campus was a depressing experience. The visitor was likely to find a flock of trainees being herded like zombies through an impossible schedule. At some places, the day's activities would begin at 6 A.M. with physical education and end at 10 P.M. with a lecture. Every moment of those hours was filled with activities dictated from above. The trainee had less autonomy than a college freshman. He was bedded in a dormitory, tumbled out at an arbitrary hour, fed in a prescribed place at a prescribed time. He hardly had time to sleep, far less to think. It was like boot camp.

Most of the trainee's days were spent being lectured at. Often the lectures were sublimely irrelevant to the environment into which the trainees were going; the lecturers spoke as though to students getting ready for an examination rather than to adults preparing for a job. This did not really matter, since the trainees were too tired to listen to what the lecturer was saying. Trainees learned to sleep with their eyes open. Because of a formless fear of sending young Americans into strange lands filled with enemy propaganda, trainees going to villages where the name of Karl Marx was unknown were subjected to speeches on the evils of communism. Health lecturers instructed the trainees in how to remain sanitized in a dirty environment, although their instructions were impossible to carry out in practice. (Statistics soon showed that the Jeep was a far greater hazard to volunteers than any bug.) In stressing the physical dangers awaiting them overseas, instead of the psychological stress of a foreign culture, health training served to perpetuate the "mud-hut" myth of the Peace Corps.

Job training was usually poor or misdirected or both. Trainees who were going to teach for the first time in their lives were given lectures on education — but no practice teaching. Others were taught the wrong skills: colorful stories soon circulated of volunteers arriving to teach people how to do something the wrong way. The critical area of language was given only perfunctory attention at first. Trainees headed for "English-speaking"

Africa got no language instruction at all, though lack of the local language was bound to cut them off from the great non-English-speaking majority of people in their new communities.

Physical education, on the other hand, was a standard feature of training and unexpectedly valuable, though not for its intended purpose. Healthy young Americans did not need any conditioning for jobs that, in terms of physical energy, proved to be more indolent than arduous. But physical education was the only break in the endless routine of passive learning. As such, it was a lifesaver for many a bored and sleepy trainee.

Hovering over the trainee was selection. This process was largely in the hands of psychologists and psychiatrists, and the specter of the "shrink" was never far from the trainee. One trainee, asked by a visitor why she refused to state her opinions in class, replied: *"They'll think I have a negative attitude."* Sensing that the Peace Corps, through the psychologists, was prying into their psyches, trainees were suspicious of everyone. The level of tension, as a result, was very high, which created a poor environment for learning. Ironically, most of this prying proved to be pointless, for there was little or no correlation between the psychologists' ratings of the trainees and their actual performance overseas.

The contrast between training and the Peace Corps experience overseas was glaring in those early days. The agency shipped volunteers out into a world where they were cut off from expert advice, where life was slow and where they carved out their roles under conditions of great uncertainty and ambiguity. Yet training, with its rigid discipline and ordering of every minute, treated them like high-school dropouts who must be watched constantly lest they slip off to the pool hall. The trainees, most of them grateful to be out of the cocoon of college, found themselves thrust back into another cocoon with less power of decision, less adult status, than they had in the one they had just left. Fortunately for the volunteers and the Peace Corps, however, training turned out to be less crucial than the agency had thought. It was, after all, only three months out of a lifetime. Most people who join the Peace Corps have already demonstrated that they can survive seventeen years of instruction that is often trivial and boring without losing their creative spirit. Another three months was not fatal; they survived that too.

Many failings of early Peace Corps training were doubtless inevitable. Everyone was groping; nothing quite like this had ever been tried before. If the psychologists chose volunteers by the standards of middle-class America instead of those of the job overseas, it was in part because that was what their selection methods were designed for; and if no one told them how to do it differently, it was because no one was quite sure what should be the measure of volunteer selection. In the case of the more exotic Peace Corps destinations, literally no language instruction was available in the United States. If the lecturers were irrelevant, no one knew where to find the relevant ones, if indeed any existed. If the instructional methods were aimed at solitary, competitive achievement, few people in the United States had tackled the task of discovering techniques for cooperative, group learning. Not much information had come back in yet from the field; and what information existed was often lost in the maze of the agency's own bureaucratic disorder.

The overstuffed schedule was the result of everyone's desire for the trainees to learn as much as possible in the brief time of training. Each official plugged for more hours for his specialty. Since the number of days was limited, the hours in the day had to be lengthened. Nothing could be cut, because everything was essential. The result was self-defeating: exhausted, overwatched, tense and suspicious, the trainees learned less than they might have with a lighter schedule. The strain on the trainees was further increased by a subtle testing and molding on the part of everyone on the staff side. The additional strain was supplied in part by the missionary mystique; no one, no matter how agnostic, could seem to shake it off the Peace Corps venture. These young Americans (as they were constantly being addressed, even though almost every departing group contained gray heads) were going into the outer darkness to save the benighted. As they assumed the magical powers to do so, they had to be tested. Rites of initiation are never painless.

The deeper problem lay in the profoundly differing attitudes and goals of the academic establishment and the Peace Corps. At first, of course, the Peace Corps had no clearly defined idea of what it wanted from its university contractors. So the university provided its usual product: it did what it already knew how to do. As time went on, people in the Peace Corps, themselves out of the academic mold, came to realize that the academic product was largely irrelevant to the agency's needs.

Just because a university had, say, a department of Latin American studies did not mean it was qualified to prepare volunteers to work in Latin America. The university does not prepare students for action — that is not its business. Since the university's original purpose, to prepare scholars to function in their field, still sets the academic tone, most of higher education is concerned with acquiring information and the verbal skills needed to capitalize on that information. "Most 'educational institutions' concern themselves with little more than assisting in their students' general intellectual development and in developing in them minor mastery of a narrow skill," John R. Seeley of Brandeis University commented. "They do little or nothing to assist students in discovering their point of engagement with and line of action in the world enterprise of their day." In place of action, the academy values emotional detachment and rational understanding. It is only appropriate then that the student is evaluated through written and verbal tests and reports — never on his ability to apply his learning in a situation requiring his commitment. Seeley deplored the separation of study and action in these terms: "It is a post-Renaissance heresy that somehow knowledge exists apart from the life into which it enters, and that life exists in a medium other than the knowing of it."

After a study of Peace Corps training, Roger Harrison of the National Training Laboratories set out some of the basic differences between the goals of academic education and the needs of people going to work overseas.*

In communication, Harrison wrote, the academic

* See "The Design of Cross-cultural Training" by Harrison and Richard Hopkins (*Journal of Applied Behavioral Science*, Vol. 3, No. 4).

goal is "to communicate fluently via the written word, and, to a lesser extent, to speak well . . . to understand readily the reasoning, the ideas and the knowledge of the other [person]." But in overseas work, says Harrison, the goal is to "understand and communicate directly and often nonverbally through movement, facial expression, person-to-person action. To listen with sensitivity to the hidden concerns, values, motives of the other. To be at home in the exchange of feelings, attitudes, desires, fears."

In decision-making, the academic goal is "to develop critical judgment: the ability to test assertions, assumptions and opinions against the hard facts and the criteria of logic . . . to be skeptical of intuition and emotion. To search for the best, most rational, most economic solution." But the goal of overseas work is "to develop ability to come to conclusions and take action on inadequate, unreliable and conflicting information. To be able to trust feelings, attitudes and beliefs as well as facts. To search for the possible course, the viable alternative, the durable though inelegant solution."

Commitment, in the academic environment, is "to truth. It requires an ability to stand back from ongoing events in order to understand and analyze them . . ." But for the volunteer overseas, "commitment is to people and relationships. It requires an ability to become involved: to be able to give and inspire trust and confidence . . ." Goals in the all-important area of problem-solving also differ, Harrison wrote. In the academic world, "a problem is solved when the true, correct, reasonable answer has been discovered and verified. Problem-solving is a search for knowledge and truth. It is a largely rational process, involving intelligence, creativity, insight and a respect for facts." But for the volunteer working overseas "a problem is solved when decisions are made and carried out which effectively apply people's energies to overcoming some barrier to a common goal. Problem-solving is a social process involving communication, interpersonal influence, consensus and commitment."

Most volunteers have just come off a campus where they absorbed academic goals and were taught the academic way of learning from established authorities (duly named in the footnotes). As Harrison points out, this method of learning "tends to create a dependency on experts and authorities." Overseas the volunteer is deprived of his authorities, and he is, therefore, in the position of "having to develop a whole new learning style pretty much on his own and unaided." This is a common observation about volunteers in the field, especially in their early months. They want to learn about their new communities, but they have no idea how to go about it — there is no library in town and no department of anthropology. In dozens of conversations all over the Peace Corps world, we have heard volunteers express great curiosity about their environment, and equally great bewilderment about how to satisfy that curiosity, though often the answers are there for the asking (if not the reading), right down the street. When Peace Corps training is conducted along conventional academic lines, it reinforces the methods of learning that the volunteer has already absorbed — and contributes to his unhappiness overseas when he finds that the method no longer works.

Only gradually did the Peace Corps perceive the depth of the gulf between what the university offered and what the agency needed. Something was wrong, however. This was obvious from the howls of protest echoing back to Washington from volunteers in the field. Training was the focus of the most bitter criticism from volunteers and to some extent from the overseas staff. Many volunteers felt they had wasted their time and had been insulted by the training institution. "The worst thing about my training was that it ever happened," one volunteer said.

Soon the Peace Corps began visibly groping toward a new concept of preparation for overseas service. The early changes in training were largely negative: they consisted of getting rid of some of what existed. The schedule was lightened (in some places; at any given time there is an extraordinary variety of practices among the Peace Corps training contractors). The number of lectures was reduced; the message got out to the universities that lecturing alone was not enough. The aimless instruction in the perils of communism was dropped as a separate component from most training programs. Some of the institutions that were most unwilling to change lost their contracts.

Among the positive changes, probably the most important was the increased emphasis on language. In 1963, the hours devoted to language were increased. Under the direction of Allan Kulakow, the agency's chief of language training, the Peace Corps began to insist on more effective teaching methods and a higher level of achievement before volunteers went overseas. In the process, the nation's ability to teach foreign languages was significantly increased, for a large proportion of the one hundred and fifty languages required by the Peace Corps were being taught for the first time in the United States.

The whole tone of training was undergoing a change through the increasing use of returned volunteers. At first, the veterans had little or no power in the training program: by academic standards, the fact that they had just returned from two years in the nation for which the trainees were bound mattered less than their lack of an advanced degree. Gradually, and in part under pressure from the Peace Corps, some training institutions began to give the returnees a larger part, and they in turn gave the training increased realism. One of the more successful educational experiments of the Peace Corps was a week-long period of training for returnees who were going to work in training programs. The small investment in the learning of discussion-leading techniques paid off handsomely.

More radical change was harder to implement. The Peace Corps wanted to place trainees in situations where they would undergo some of the stress of overseas. In coping with that stress, the trainees would learn by doing, and they would learn with their emotions rather than with their reason alone. The experience would serve to break the trainees out of the college mold. But it was clear that a college classroom was hardly the place to undo the habits learned in a lifetime in classrooms.

With considerable boldness, Peace Corps contractors began plunging trainees into the outside world. There are plenty of places in the United States or nearby where middle-class Americans can be put into an environment uncomfortably different from their own. Some trainees were put on Indian reservations for part of their training. Perhaps the most profound encounter took place when sheltered white trainees were put into the other America of our urban Negro ghettoes. Often they were required to find their own housing in the ghetto, even to find a nominal job they could work at — usually some sort of volunteer service — for a month or two. This was done in a program training a large group of teachers for Sierra Leone, run by ex-volunteer Robert McGuire, in Washington in 1967. The dispersion of trainees in the Washington ghetto resulted in some chaos; but it also supplied an environment for the trainees in which their ability to survive was sorely tested. Sometimes the universities, themselves frightened of the slums, only dangled the trainees in the ghetto environment rather than immersing them in it to sink or swim. Even in these cases, however, enough happened to prove the worth of the technique. In the slums of Miami, girls training for public health did the rounds with the local public health nurses, seeing the many patterns of ghetto resistance to outsiders, observing the success or failure of differing approaches by the nurses. Trainees for an English teaching program were sent for their practice teaching to a Catholic school in Quebec. No one in the school spoke English, the kids were hard to handle, and the conservative attitude of the faculty provided a healthy cross-cultural dose for the trainees.

The experience of another culture was worthwhile in training even when that culture bore no relation to the overseas assignments, the Peace Corps believed. What really mattered was that trainees undergo an encounter

with people whose way of life was different from their
own. In summer, 1966, trainees were working evenings
in a community center in a black ghetto of Atlanta. The
scene was out of the third world. It was hot, noisy,
crowded, intimate, disorganized. In one corner an elderly
illiterate was being tutored by a trainee; over here some
girls in their early teens were dancing to an ancient Gram-
ophone; in the next room was the beginning of a camera
club. Supposedly the trainees' jobs were arranged in
advance, but they arrived to find the center in disarray
(the same sort of chaos they would find in their jobs
overseas). The more courageous trainees had ventured
out into the ghetto community and had found its in-
fluentials; through them, they had managed to get a series of activities going at the center. "When I go see old
Mrs. Jones we drink beer and eat pigs' feet for an hour
or so before she'll get down to the business at hand, but
that's the way it's done here," one Northern white
trainee commented. "I kind of like it," he added as an
afterthought, grinning. He was a long, long way from the
college classroom, a journey symbolic of the distance the
Peace Corps had come in its thinking about training
for work overseas.

Other reforms were aimed at increasing the trainees'
ability to communicate on the level of attitude and emotion. In many programs, the technique of sensitivity
training was used to heighten the trainees' awareness of
themselves as seen by others, so that they could better
perceive what people overseas would see when they
looked at the American newcomer. Group dynamics
training was added to teach trainees to perceive how they
interacted with groups of their peers and how groups, as

well as individuals, could become functioning wholes.
The trend generally was toward loosening up the schedule, giving the trainees more power to make decisions,
more time to decide whether they and the Peace Corps
were cut out for each other.

The new wave in training reached its peak in projects designed by Richard Hopkins at the Puerto Rico
center. Trainees were given almost total responsibility
for their own learning, the boldest move yet. Outside
experts were brought in, and always there were returned
volunteers with specific skills and area expertise close at
hand to give advice or comments when asked. But they
would speak only when spoken to. The staff burst forth
with paroxysms of inventiveness. "Two hundred fifty
baby chicks are arriving in the morning," they would
tell the trainees. "What are you going to do with them?"
For many trainees, the transition from the super-coddled
college environment was too much. But most made
good headway, despite the fact that the staff could have
done a more competent job of winnowing out the necessary from the unnecessary learning experiences. The
Puerto Rico experiments did not last due to gusts of
terror that blew through Peace Corps headquarters.
Nonetheless, they opened the way for many similar
ventures in the universities.

In various ways, trainees were introduced to methods
of learning that they could apply overseas. Some institutions sent them out to do community surveys. One
of the most systematic approaches was that of Michigan
State University, which trained volunteers for community development in Latin America in the holistic method
outlined in Chapter 6. The trainees learned a detailed

method of field research and planning before going for three weeks to temporary sites in the back country of Mexico. At the sites, they developed plans for what they would do were they to be community development workers there. They kept a written record of their findings. They then evaluated their work with their instructors. During training they scrupulously avoided initiating projects, recognizing that they were only visitors in their temporary sites. Thus, before these volunteers left for overseas they had gone through an exercise similar to what other volunteers were going through in the field.

This was training for the kind of action research which, as we have seen in earlier chapters, is the base for so many successful Peace Corps enterprises. The agency has also made attempts to motivate volunteers to continue to learn systematically once overseas. In keeping with the academic distinction between "work" and "study," many volunteers stopped any real effort to learn once they were at their sites. Instead of maintaining a learner's role for the twenty-four months of their service, such volunteers felt that once their "working" period arrived their time for "study" was over. The evidence seems to show that volunteers trained in a method of action research are more likely to go on learning in the field. It may also be that a plunge into the task of researching their new communities helps volunteers survive those difficult early months of confrontation with a strange environment.

Since the purpose of many of the new techniques was to expose the trainees to the environment they would be entering, it seemed logical to provide the real thing — that is, to send them to the country in which they were to serve for training. The Peace Corps began to experiment with giving volunteers part of their training overseas. In India, which had plenty of facilities available, in-country training proved to be a success; volunteers later said they learned more faster in India than in the first part of their training, which had been conducted in the United States. But in-country training has been inhibited by the expense of paying the voyage home of trainees who drop out, or are dropped, overseas.

Recently the role of the Peace Corps-operated centers has increased, causing some observers to forecast the day when the last foothold of private organizations would be lost. The Virgin Islands center began to do carefully designed training for cross-cultural involvement in Africa.* Puerto Rico began to dabble in the kind of group dynamics work which formed the basis of the VESPRA program described in Chapter 6. People at a Hawaii training center envisioned establishing, at long last, a sort of "Peace Corps Academy" for East Asia and the Pacific. A new Peace Corps-run center was opened near San Diego. With ample reserves of Spanish speakers nearby, this center hoped to do a more effective job of training in action research and planning — not only for aspiring Latin America volunteers, but for the staff as well.

These were the main lines of new thinking by the Peace Corps about training. That thinking was not shared by many universities, and even in the agency many people found the more far-out innovations too radical for their taste. Failure to change was at times

---

* The method used in the Virgin Islands is described in *Preparation for Encounter* by Phillips Ruopp and Paul Wrobel.

the fault of the Peace Corps rather than the university. Some bold ideas coming out of the academy were rejected in Washington; the agency has sometimes turned down innovation because of the high cost it usually involves; and some promising institutions have given up on the Peace Corps because of the extraordinarily exasperating process of negotiating contracts with an agency that niggles over the tiniest detail and yet lives in bureaucratic disorder. The rate at which the innovations have been put into practice has therefore been uneven. Because of the high turnover in Peace Corps employees and in training institutions there has also been a high turnover in ideas as well. Indeed, Peace Corps training is so widely dispersed that it is hard to get a clear picture of what is going on at any one time. However, the partnership between American higher education and the Peace Corps must have been showing cracks at the seams. In the summer of 1967 Brent Ashabranner, deputy director of the agency, urged restraint by both parties so as to get past the itchy seventh year of the partnership. What Ashabranner may have known was that in academia rising irritation with the Johnson administration was being expressed, perhaps not entirely consciously, as hostility toward the Peace Corps.

Old-fashioned training programs of strictly academic content and irrelevance undoubtedly still exist. In summer, 1966, it was still possible to find, for instance, a doctor instructing trainees that, when required for social reasons to eat food that might be unsanitary, they should promptly go outside and vomit! The old and the new could even be found side by side on the same campus. One university in 1966 ran two programs for Africa teachers from separate offices. In space, the two programs were only a few blocks apart, but in evolution they were separated by what seemed like an ice age. One program was a throwback to the early days of the Peace Corps-university connection; the other embodied many of the new ideas we have described. In the first project, a visitor was told with some pride that at this university training was being conducted by "expert-experts." These rare birds turned out to be doctors of education with no African experience; to preserve harmony and hierarchy returned volunteers were kept on the sidelines. When the visitor asked if the textbook being used by the "experts" was the one used in African schools, the answer was: "No — but it could be used in Africa." The trainees were forced to write papers; they were tested by written examinations. Visiting lecturers told them about Africa, but an outsider could never have guessed the trainees were going to teach; the unfocused lectures could have been aimed at State Department people or airline stewardesses. The visitor asked a trainee what she thought about the school-leavers in Nigeria (where she was going), easily that troubled country's most discussed educational problem. "You mean l-e-v-e-r-s?" she asked. "Never heard of them!"

Up the street the scene was dramatically different. Returned volunteer teachers were conducting the training. They used the textbooks and curriculum of the African schools, and the trainees were already familiar with the all-important examination that their future pupils would have to face. The returnees were showing the recruits how to teach imaginatively within the existing strictures of the African system, how to be creative and still prepare their pupils for the examination; and the returnees were doing all this using the very methods they advocated. The science teacher taught field trips by taking the trainees on field trips; he deliberately mismanaged one trip and let the trainees figure out what had gone wrong. The English teacher was forcing the trainees to uncover and examine those American attitudes about grammar which he had found were the greatest handicap in teaching the language to African children. The trainees were alert, challenged, participating. Their attention was focused, not on Africa as a vague generality, but on the schools in which they would succeed or fail.

That a few institutions are still doing what came naturally in 1961 should not obscure the extent of the changes that have occurred. Considering the innate conservatism of any educational system, it is surprising how much innovation has taken place, how many steps — at times stumbling and uncertain — have been taken toward a new kind of preparation for Americans who go overseas. The training connection between the Peace Corps and the universities is all that remains of the original determination to make the agency into a partnership with the private sector. The universities' share of the pie might have been immense if, at one time, they had been interested in combining their training with overseas administration contracts. According to Thomas Scott, writing in the *Annals of the American Academy of Political and Social Science* (May, 1966), universities could have provided most of the overseas administration as well as training in the early years, administration which the Peace Corps itself often badly bumbled with untrained staff. The universities, according to Scott, "failed to do so for a variety of reasons. First, their desire to participate was sated early by the decision to contract almost all Peace Corps volunteer training to the American colleges. Second, many were genuinely reluctant to get into operations overseas, feeling . . . . with Rowland Eggers . . . that they were 'better at writing history, than making it.' "*

Even if only a fraction of the ideas and innovations we have described here has actually been put into practice in the average training program, the Peace Corps would still emerge as a force for change in American higher education. Even if the agency were to disappear tomorrow, any future training for overseas would be influenced by the results of the Peace Corps experience. Its most practical effect has been to increase the universities' capacity to teach foreign languages and to encourage a new look into the study of other nations. Returned volunteers in graduate school have been an important lobby for a more realistic approach to studying other societies. But the potential influence of the Peace Corps is far broader: the innovations it has promoted are relevant to education for life in the United States as well as overseas. Educational innovators have received the support of hard cash. At most of the institutions with Peace Corps contracts, some campus decision makers have been forced into contact with one or another of the new methods. Some new ideas have been put in circulation, some fresh air let into the classroom. (An entertaining case of fresh, and not entirely welcome air brought by the Peace Corps occurred when

* Thomas Scott was intimately involved, as a Peace Corps employee, in trying to maintain contact with the private sector. He is the only writer, to our knowledge, to have delivered an unflattering yet accurate account of the evolution of the "other" Peace Corps — the nonvolunteer part of the agency with which we deal only sketchily in this book.

a training contract was signed with a strait-laced Southern Negro college. On that provincial church-ridden campus, where students were forced to button up starchily in coats and ties on Sunday, the trainees, most of them from the North, came on like a bunch of far-out swingers. "Why can't we wear shorts like Peace Corps girls?" a student complained in the cafeteria, and another student announced that the Peace Corps example had inspired him to start a movement for greater student freedom.)

The effort to break down the barrier between "study" and "work," between thought and action, is the most significant aspect of the Peace Corps participation in higher education. As we have stated before, the Peace Corps can only be viewed in the context of present-day America. If the agency has been surprisingly daring in its support for educational pioneering, it is because the climate in recent years has been favorable to change. A decade ago it would have been hard to imagine, for example, that any federal agency would have even considered sending recruits for overseas service into American urban ghettoes. The universities themselves have been re-examining their role in society, and many of them have been moving along the same lines of thought as the Peace Corps. Some academics have come to believe that a system originally designed to instruct upper-class youth and to train scholars is outmoded now that the college population has multiplied and scholarship can be the future occupation of only a tiny minority. Some believe the old system, and its attendant withdrawn intellectualism, are no longer applicable to the electronic age.

The greatest pressure for change has, of course, come

from the students themselves. In keeping with the spirit of the times, students have been trying to break out of the campus ghetto and make contact with the world. Within the campus, they have been seeking a greater voice in the process for which they are paying such high fees. Sometimes this has been through a dramatic rebellion, like that at Berkeley. But even the middle-of-the-road National Student Association, while shaking off its CIA connection, let loose a call for "student power." The student desire for participation is similar to the Peace Corps goal of giving trainees a deciding voice in their training and, beyond that, to the role of the volunteer overseas in aiding people to gain for themselves greater power over their environment.

Through its training contracts, and indirectly through returning volunteers and staff members, the Peace Corps has taken part in the movement for a new philosophy of education. Roger Harrison believes that it will be in such sidelines as Peace Corps training that ". . . the experiments will be conducted and the innovations tested which will determine the form of tomorrow's colleges and universities." That prediction, fondly shared as a hope by many in the Peace Corps, is proving itself in at least one instance. Harris Wofford, one of the greatest of the agency's earlier idea men, left the Peace Corps to become president of a new college at Old Westbury, Long Island, part of the New York State University system, dedicated to experiment and innovation. If people like Wofford prove Harrison to be right, then Peace Corps training at its best is a precursor of a kind of higher education that is attuned to the world of today and tomorrow rather than to the artifacts of yesterday.

chapter **8**

THE AGENT OF CHANGE

Chronicles of frustration and failure in the Peace Corps are common, but something that looks like success also appears. For a long time the Peace Corps tended to call successful anyone who gritted his teeth and hung on for two years. As the effects of overseas programs (as against the mere expenditure of volunteer effort) became a legitimate topic for scrutiny, it began to be apparent that the job of the volunteer contained more than just brute determination to survive. The following excerpts from the overseas record may help to point up some elements usually present in the "golden 10 percent," as old Peace Corps hands sometimes call the agency's instances of apparent effectiveness.

Teaching. In one African nation there is a school system which provides a refreshing change from the type described in Chapter 3. This country is Tanzania, and the school system covers the upper primary grades;

the Peace Corps volunteers have taught in the equivalent of grades 7 and 8. The students were twelve to fifteen years old. Three-quarters of them did not go on to further education. But, in contrast to the elite schools elsewhere in Africa, most of the students did not head into a big city to seek a job. Most of them stayed in their villages, where they had a priceless opportunity to act as agents of rural change. The Peace Corps volunteers lived and worked out in the bush in a pleasantly relaxed setting. Rules were flexible, and the administrative disorder of the upper primary gave the volunteer both freedom and opportunity. His colleagues were non-elite Africans — easier to work with than Europeans or higher-level Africans.* So were the students who, in the words of Stanley Meisler, a former Peace Corps Africa specialist, "are not like the secondary school students who are convinced that life has no more meaning than a starched white collar and a red Mercedes." One volunteer got his students to work on a sisal plantation to earn money for the soccer uniforms they wanted, a proposition secondary students undoubtedly would have rejected as beneath them.

When the volunteers in upper primary schools in Tanzania tried to introduce new problem-solving teaching techniques, in place of rote learning, they had the implicit support of the nation's president, Julius Nyerere. Nyerere, who was once a teacher himself, has said: "It is no use the teachers giving to their pupils the answers to the existing problems of our nation. By the

---

* In his book, *An African Season*, former volunteer Leonard Levitt gives a sensitive description of his experience in a Tanzanian school.

time the pupils are adults, the problems will have changed." Nyerere's point of view is all too rare in the third world, even in his own nation's secondary schools. For a time the Peace Corps was able to participate on a level where new approaches to teaching could pay off, and where volunteers could live and work in the context of Tanzania's real needs. At one time almost two hundred volunteers were so involved, not only in teaching the full range of primary school subjects, but also in creating opportunities for extra-curricular activities for their students, such as sports programs and special-interest clubs. Stanley Meisler commented: "Statistics by themselves do not prove anything, but it has become clear that the poorer nations cannot develop on the strength of a skilled managerial class alone. They also need a . . . population with alertness and initiative, a desire for change, and some hope for it. In Tanzania, the primary schools can possibly do the job of equipping many non-elite Tanzanians with these qualities."

An interesting coda to the Tanzania school story: in 1967 Nyerere decided to eliminate all foreigners from primary schools. Thus the Peace Corps program was due to be closed down. Nyerere's reasons for this move are perhaps the same reasons why many countries did not want Peace Corps volunteers (or other foreigners) in their schools in the first place. At any event, Nyerere is not near the top of the State Department's list of Africa's most pliable leaders; his, and his nation's, attitude toward Americans was strongly influenced by the CIA revelations of 1967 and the American military adventure in Southeast Asia. The case of the Tanzanian upper primary schools provides an example of how the

Peace Corps finds a chance to work in an effective job for a short time, then has to withdraw for reasons beyond its control. In Tanzania, the close relationships that developed between volunteers and headmasters were clues that a profitable partnership had existed. Volunteers were not merely trying to subvert an existing curriculum and replace it with one stamped "Made in America." They were filling a need — often actually filling vacant teaching posts — where their ability to innovate was limited only by their ability to relate what they were doing to the Tanzanian students and headmasters. We can presume that the upper primary schools were better off for having had the young Americans for a time; we must also presume that not having them will not deal a mortal blow to the system. There was a potentially important side effect. Based in part, at least, on the Peace Corps experience, Tanzania was trying to develop its own national youth service to put university students out in the bush to teach.

Rural action. John is a volunteer assigned to a remote village in South India. John, and other members of his Peace Corps group, were tossed into one of the harshest rural environments in the world: the arid bosom of Mother India. An Indian village is crowded, cramped and all too unsmiling a place; as you walk around, you are constantly aware of scrawny bodies and apathetic faces. Riven by caste and class, the village has a ghetto where the untouchables are kept in strict segregation ("Just like home . . ." a volunteer remarked sardonically.) The village can have a stifling effect on the outsider. John lived in an adobe house, provided by a local farmer, that had neither electricity nor running water — but was still infinitely better than the tiny hovels most villagers call home. John had no privacy; his involvement with his new neighbors lasted twenty-four hours a day. At any time of day or night, Indians streamed through his house, examining his goods or staring silently at the visitor; Indians slept on his front steps. "By evening everyone in the village knows exactly what I had for lunch," he said. John felt he must obey the rigid taboos of Hinduism. He ate no meat in that vegetarian community ("When I get to the city, I order two dinners and eat only the meat . . ."). Alcohol was taboo, so John drank no beer. With the endless prying of villagers around his household, John felt any secreted meat or booze would soon be discovered — and he would lose standing in village eyes. Hospitality cannot be refused. In villagers' homes, he ate their fiery and unsanitary curry; periodically John came down with dysentery.

If John's life was circumscribed, his job was not. He was almost completely free to make a job for himself — or not to do anything. His vague assignment was to help the village farmers make use of the "package" of new farm practices offered by government services, none of which was located in the village. His Indian superior, the local agricultural agent, was in a town two hours' distance by bicycle; he seldom if ever came to John's village. A Peace Corps staff member might come by once in three months or so. If John wanted to sleep away his days, no one would prevent it; no one outside the village was likely even to know it. What he did when he went out of his house in the morning was entirely up to John; what he accomplished depended on his inventiveness and on the relations he was able to work out with the village farmers.

John's main contact was his "host" farmer, who provided his house and who lived a few steps away. The farmer was well off by Indian standards. He owned about forty acres of land, far above average in over-crowded India. He seemed to prefer leisure to money. He hired landless laborers, the poorest of India's poor, to work his land while he devoted as little time as possible to his fields. His crops, sorghum and millet, are tough local varieties that can be grown with little care.

"John's land" was an acre that the farmer was letting him use for the purpose of demonstrating hybrid corn under irrigation. The farmer provided John with laborers as well. The farmer was skeptical about the Indian Government's "package" of agricultural improvements. He let John use that acre because he could afford the loss of its production, and perhaps to please the young foreigner. He may well have been skeptical also of John's abilities as a farmer. Like the great majority of his Peace Corps group, John grew up on asphalt and studied liberal arts in college. He knew nothing of agriculture when he joined the Peace Corps and did not know much when he arrived in the village; his rich New York accent sounded incongruous in that rustic setting.

Although John was no farmer, he could help the Indian farmer in areas where they were both learning. One project was trying to instruct the laborers in the land leveling needed to control irrigation water. John didn't know much about leveling, but since irrigation is new, neither did the farmer and the laborers. Coming from a culture where change is familiar, John learned fast, and his interest was a stimulus to a farmer who had no other ready source of information about irrigation or all the other complexities of modern agriculture. John had also helped some local farmers in dealing with the world outside their village. The crops of several farmers, including his host, were endangered because another farmer up the irrigation canal was hogging the limited supply of water. The farmers complained among themselves, but were not about to do anything, since the water hog was richer than any one of them. John suggested they form a committee and jointly petition the government office in charge of the irrigation works. The idea was novel to the farmers, but they agreed to it, and their petition succeeded in getting the office to take action against the water hog.

John and other volunteers in his group were serving as a channel to convey grass-roots criticism to the distant officials who make the decisions concerning the "package" program. One volunteer working in a seed-processing plant, the only one in the region, reported that the plant was providing the farmers with spoiled seed — a sure way to discredit the whole program. Others were telling officials of the government that farmers in their villages were losing money on the new hybrid sorghum that the government was promoting. Of course the volunteers were not competent to design a remedy to the sorghum problem, but they were performing the essential first step of making the officials aware that a problem existed. Meanwhile, John and others in India like him were making those small daily discoveries about the rural environment that can only come from total immersion in India and from close observation.

Public Health. In 1966 Peggy Anderson, a Peace Corps staff member, visited the African country of Niger, where volunteers were working in a health pro-

gram largely designed by a physician on the Peace Corps
staff in the country, Dr. David Nicholas. Nicholas believed that nonspecialists could be valuable in public
health work; he once said: "If you can teach public
health to a Nigerien mother, you ought to be able to
teach it to a volunteer generalist."

Research performed by Dr. Nicholas sparked the
efforts of the fifteen Peace Corps girls stationed in un-
dermanned dispensaries in remote towns. Nicholas had
found that the country had an ample supply of protein
in the adult diet but that many people nonetheless
showed the symptoms of protein deficiency. He observed that the deficiency occurred mainly in the brief
period between six months of age and two years, after
the mother's milk had become insufficient in protein
and before the baby got solid protein food. Though the
time was short, the damage was often lifelong. Nicholas
then developed a protein-rich baby food made of cheap,
locally available ingredients. The volunteers were trying
to introduce this food in their communities.

Miss Anderson was able to see the results. Action-
oriented research along the lines described in Chapter
4 was the key to the volunteers' promising start in Niger.
She reported that:

These volunteers have found out a tremendous
amount about their communities and thus about doing
public health in Niger, and that is the single most important reason for their success.

Nicholas deserves much of the credit for getting the
girls started in this research. He has them spend the first
two or three months in their towns just learning; they

observe at the dispensaries, they work on improving their language, they get to know the town and the people and the power structure, and they find out all they can about health. At the end of this learning period, the volunteers send Nicholas a report describing the local health situation and outlining their plans for a public health program. It is impossible to read these initial reports without being amazed at how much the volunteers are able to find out in a very short time. A particularly impressive (but by no means unusual) study, which came from Linda Ewing and Mary Blanford after their first two months in Tessaoua, goes on for 14 typed, single-spaced pages and includes, beside a rundown on the volunteers' activities since their arrival and their plans, a section on the economy of Tessaoua; a section on local sanitation problems; a discussion of diseases prevalent in Tessaoua; a description of Hausa medicines and treatments; a discussion of local diet; a description of local weaning customs; and tables showing what foods are available in what seasons, where they can be found (market, shops, gardens, private vendors, or growing wild), and how much they cost.

Other volunteers' reports include "Personal Hygiene and the Environmental Sanitation of the Hausa People in Magaria" . . . "Health Superstitions among the Traditional Hausa" . . . and "Hausa Witch-doctors and their Medical Treatments" . . .

In considering these reports, it is important to remember that we're not talking about anthropologists or medical doctors on research grants or experts on Africa, but about a French major from Dallas, a political science major from Wooster, and other generalists, most of whom had never set foot in Africa or written a word on personal hygiene anywhere. Their impressive store of knowledge stands them in sharp relief to the technicians of the now bygone T. project [described in Chapter 5], who hung success on their skills rather than on an understanding of the local scene.

"If the Peace Corps public health project in Niger ever fails," Miss Anderson concluded, "it will be because the volunteers couldn't *solve* the problems, not because they didn't *see* them."

Community development. A volunteer in Colombia, whose natural bent led him to study the process of development, created what seemed to be a new kind of experiment. This volunteer, Jim Iszler, spent his first few months in the Peace Corps trying valiantly to make a success of a garden project designed to improve the nutrition of peasants. At one point he and a Colombian friend who became an ally sat down and calculated what they might be able to do in a year. At best, they figured, they could get twenty successful gardens going. "Small peas," Iszler wrote later in describing his work, "when you take into consideration our year full-time, the number of people in the area, and the results for the peasant even if a garden project is successful — so what, he eats cauliflower while his cows go unvaccinated, he drinks unboiled and contaminated water, he lives with chickens and pigs in his house, and does not have a bed to sleep on."

Iszler and his Colombian friend next tried to follow the established community development pattern used by Tony in Blanquita (see Chapter 6) — Acción Comunal. After a few months they found that they had assumed the role of errand boys — getting the materials for bridges, schools and other structures, and wasting large amounts of time cajoling local officials or skeptical groups of peasants. Every so often they were able to help a local community development committee get something visible built. Iszler wrote: "Someone said the bridge is not important, it's the idea of people working together that counts. I don't exactly go along with that. After the bridge is built and the celebration is over, they all go home and nothing happens until *they* decide to work together again. I question the effectiveness of an outsider trying to make people feel their needs!"

The key to investing time and effort most effectively came to Iszler and his Colombian ally only after a year of diverse attempts at community development. At this point they decided to organize short seminars for peasants. Participants would be elected by the various communities in the region. The seminars would be held in a central location and would provide training in leadership skills as well as simplified, adapted technology related to rural life. Iszler's own efforts were split between visiting rural communities to explain the courses (so as to assure that the villagers would select a member of their community who would command respect upon his return) and organizing the courses themselves. He felt strongly that no one could teach a Colombian better than another Colombian; to this end, he rounded up a wide variety of trained people who were willing to donate their time to the seminars. Without having to reach outside the region he was able to recruit a doctor and a public health nurse, a veterinarian, an agronomist, three nutritionists, a specialist on cooperatives, and an Acción Comunal man to teach classes in community

development. The Colombian Army furnished quarters
and food plus courses in defense against bandits, in return for the admission of a few soldiers to each seminar.

Looking back on the seminars later, Iszler said that
in some of the communities which had sent participants
to the seminars "there was just about no noticeable
change. In others, however, [the program] changed the
whole economy of the area. Classes were being given to
adults each Sunday in schoolhouses, gardens were planted,
fruit trees sprayed, etc. One man came home from the
seminar so excited about gardens that he planted and
cared for about three acres of tomatoes. The seminar
actually changed the whole economy of his little farm."
Iszler and his Colombian friend extended the effect of
the seminars by getting other Peace Corps volunteers
and Colombians to do follow-up work in communities
that had participated, which, it turned out, were eager
to use any new information that the outsiders could
bring them. Iszler estimated that the effectiveness of
the program in such cases was double that where no
follow-up work could be done. One of the most surprising effects of the seminars was on the educated Colombians who participated as teachers. "Almost all of
them," Iszler reported, "told me they probably had
learned more than the peasants. Certainly they left the
courses with a much better understanding of the problems and beliefs of the peasants. Most of the teachers
were disappointed a seminar didn't last longer because
it gave them a chance to have daily contact with the
people they should really have been working with, without having to go out afoot or on horseback many hours
for just a few minutes of extension work."

Iszler reported that the seminars, according to his information, began to fall to pieces a year after his departure. However, he recognized an important point: each seminar could stand on its own and justify its expense — about one hundred dollars for three weeks for thirty *campesinos* — even without detailed follow-up in the communities. In fact, realizing how easily things tend to fall apart in the third world, Iszler had planned his work as a volunteer so that it would be self-liquidating. He had hoped that Colombians could continue to operate seminars, but he didn't deceive himself that survival of the idea was guaranteed. (What he didn't know was that three years later the idea caught fire again and was blazing brightly.) Iszler had brought to his Peace Corps job an interest in the process of community development which, after a period of patient experimenting, caused him to invest his efforts in something that worked.

Interestingly enough, the idea of leadership training courses for isolated peasants blossomed several years later in the neighboring country of Ecuador; and the new venture was begun without any knowledge of Iszler's success in Colombia. It is quite possible that similar programs are producing measurable results elsewhere in Latin America, or in other parts of the world. In Senegal, to our knowledge, a much larger and better-documented program of the same sort has been in effect for some time — though without much assistance from the Peace Corps.*

These four cases illuminate some aspects of the

* See *Africa: From Independence to Tomorrow* by David Hapgood, Chapter 6.

Peace Corps job and the way the volunteers approached it. In the case of the Niger health workers and the teachers in the Tanzania upper primary schools, the setting itself was favorable from the start. John in India and Jim Iszler in Colombia, on the other hand, made favorable jobs for themselves. In all four cases the volunteers were more deeply immersed (by their job and by their own inclinations) in the foreign culture than is the average volunteer. In the Tanzania schools, the rural development effort in India and the peasant leadership seminars there was no clash with host-country institutions and little friction with local customs. Volunteers in these cases were adding something that wasn't already there to the operation of government services. Particularly in the case of Jim Iszler's seminars, there was a deliberate attempt to join what technology and skills the elite had to offer with the needs of the forgotten peasants, and to do it in such a way as to establish a two-way flow of communications. In the case of John, the same technique was at work between the villagers and their government. In three of the cases there seems to have been a kind of patience and desire to experiment until useful answers were found — in Iszler's case, a new approach to reaching the peasants; in John's, a way of helping adapt new farming technology to the reality of village India; in the nutrition girls', a corrective to protein deficiency that was cheap and locally available. Also common to all four cases is another element, perhaps the most pervasive and significant single factor in all stories of "success" in the Peace Corps. Volunteers not only lived close to the people with whom they were working — at their level, without too many of the barriers that affluence normally erects between helped and helper, and sharing their daily life in a kind of total immersion. They also deliberately investigated the locale, its customs and the resources. This action research can be either part of a formal job, as in the Niger nutrition program, or an outgrowth of necessity, as in the case of John. Local lore is not merely soaked up by osmosis; it is pursued with restless curiosity as one of the prerequisites upon which effective action must eventually be based.

The four cases we have described as having achieved some kind of success are a distinct minority (remembering that there have been some thirty thousand cases to date). The brief analysis we have applied to them is likewise far from typical: planning volunteer jobs — called "programming" — has never operated with much self-assurance in the Peace Corps. The reason, of course, is the ambiguity of Peace Corps goals: what *is* a successful volunteer, what *does* he do that distinguishes him from the unsuccessful?

No unanimous answers have been set forth by the Peace Corps. In fact, until very recently, nobody seemed interested in sitting down with case studies of volunteer effectiveness. Dr. Morris Stein's book, *Volunteers for Peace*, which tackled the question of what makes success in community development, was scarcely read in the agency. No one, it seemed, wanted to pin the Peace Corps down to objective criteria.

Peace Corps thinking on the nature of its mission — what should be measured to establish success or failure — has wobbled around over the years, often in response to the fads of social science and sometimes in *ex post facto* efforts to justify what it was already doing. The idea that the volunteers were providing technical aid that could be measured — and hopefully photographed for use in the next recruiting pamphlet — had to be played down when the volunteers turned out to be generalists without technical skills, and when the early volunteer-promoted urinals and other more photogenic monuments fell into disuse following the strangers' departure. More recently, it has become fashionable to say that the Peace Corps business is "changing attitudes." This reflects the popular belief that attitudes in the third world are an important barrier to development. But no one in the Peace Corps has defined just what attitudes need to be changed in what situations, and how the volunteers will go about doing it. In one sense, this line of thought reflects our familiar cultural imperialism, for saying you are going to change people's attitudes amounts to saying that what those people need is to become more like us — i.e., conversion to the American way of life. In another sense, those who said this may have been simply finding a convenient rationale for their failure to accomplish anything measurable. How, after all, do you prove that someone is *not* changing attitudes?

Lack of any definition of where the Peace Corps was trying to go had the advantage of allowing all sorts of experiments. Peace Corps experimentation, which has produced such awkward yet exciting programs as an educational television system in Colombia and a tuberculosis control venture in Malawi, has been one of the most attractive traits of the agency. Official statements of purpose out of Washington were usually so broad (Shriver: ". . . to permit America to participate directly, personally and effectively in this struggle for human dignity . . .") as to hamper no one's innovating spirit. Blue-sky thinking ("institution-building — that's what the Peace Corps is all about"; or Jack Vaughn's "love — that's what the Peace Corps is all about") tended to prosper when it reinforced the emotional appeal of the Peace Corps idea. Even today, few Americans visualize the Peace Corps as much more than a simple hands-across-the-ocean gesture of friendship toward brown brothers everywhere. Yet when it came to decisions about numbers of volunteers and the money needed to sustain them, some basic concepts of programming were bound to emerge. It is possible to identify two main concepts that have governed programming — two threads that reappear from the tangled web in which the agency's programmers so frequently seemed trapped.

The first concept views young Americans with a commitment to service as "good seed" to be cast abroad on foreign soil, there to sprout and grow and cast their seed in turn. The most eloquent expression of what this means comes from former Nigeria volunteer David Schickele:

My instincts revolt against the whole idea of having to prove in some mechanistic or quantitative way the value of the Peace Corps. If the aim is to help people, I understand that in the sense of the Ibo proverb which says that when the right hand washes the left hand, the right hand becomes clean also. E. M. Forster has said that "love is a great force in private life," but in public affairs "it does not work. The fact is we can only love

what we know personally, and we cannot know much.
The only thing that cuts a little ice is affection, or the
possibility of affection." I only know that when I am
infuriated by some article in a Nigerian newspaper, I can
summon up countless images of dusty cycle rides with
Paul Okpokam, reading poetry with Glory Nwanodi,
dancing and drinking palm wine with Gabriel Ogar, and
it suddenly matters very much that I go beyond my an-
noyance to some kind of understanding. That my Nigerian friends trust me is no reason for them to trust Washington or forgive Birmingham; but something is there
which was not there before and which the world is better
for having.

For some in the Peace Corps, it was not enough just
to read poetry and drink palm wine and gradually feel
that "something" begin to grow. They wanted to see
their good seed sprout and bear fruit. They wanted to
define the "something." Frank Mankiewicz, who for
two years directed the Peace Corps Latin American
programs, said:

. . . The volunteer must make immediate, physical
visible common cause with the people he is there to work
with. That means live in their village or in their slum
area. . . . To an extent, a community development
effort in Latin America is an international sit-in. . . . It
is the task of the volunteer to call attention to his frag-
mented community, to ease the sense of alienation, to
function, in short, in the best Christian sense of the word,
as a "witness" to the existence of the majority of the nation's citizens.

There is a tremendous appeal to all of this. Any person with juices flowing in his body must be drawn to a movement that talks about conducting international sit-ins, drinking palm wine and reciting poetry — and making common cause with the ordinary men and women of the developing world, living with them, bearing witness to their existence so as to bring their misery to the attention of the rich and powerful. But only a scant handful of volunteers has ever made much of a job out of this good-seed approach to helping. Few have been talented enough to keep busy, involved and communicative. The majority — and, we suspect, this is true of most sit-ins — were bored and idle even though in a good cause. Or, to confound their guilt over feeling useless, they ran amok with projects that went all the way from giving away Mickey Mouse watches (this happened) to teaching peasants how to make adobe bricks (which those peasants knew how to do to perfection already).

These volunteers were victims of an almost complete lack of planning on the part of the Peace Corps. An "international sit-in" is a tricky and complex undertaking: indeed, the promoting of change in other societies is hard to justify except on the grounds that those societies are already undergoing a massive, often destructive, assault from the developed nations. When the sit-in is launched with no definition of what it is trying to accomplish, still less how the volunteer will serve that goal, one might legitimately suspect that the sit-in urge is motivated more by the desire to "bear witness" than by the necessity to accomplish a goal relevant to the people among whom one is sitting in. Bearing witness alone, without any change in the situation witnessed, may salve the conscience of the witness, but is of little use to the people whose misery he witnessed.

The good-seed concept rests on assumptions that reflect deep-rooted American attitudes. These attitudes are the unspoken major premise that has governed much Peace Corps programming. When David Schickele mentions the Ibo proverb, his point presumably is that *his* hand, the right one, was washed in his encounter with Nigeria. This is undoubtedly true, of Schickele himself and of a great many volunteers: the encounter has been fruitful for them. But what about the left, or third-world hand? What evidence is there that the left hand really was washed in the Peace Corps encounter? Good-seed programming was grounded in blind faith that contact with the volunteers would produce some value for the people of the third world. If you peel this assumption to its core, you find a colossally ethnocentric attitude: that we Americans are so good (or skilled, or democratic, or whatever) that our very presence among the less fortunate is a benefit in itself. The innocent arrogance of this American attitude has flawed much that the Peace Corps has done, and it still colors the agency's policies. Although random broadcasting of volunteers has greatly decreased, the good-seed assumption made itself felt when, about 1966, agency planners began to wrestle seriously with the complex question of how to measure volunteer effectiveness overseas. The main measure being considered then was a tabulation of the number of contacts between volunteers and the people they work with. Virtually nothing was said about the nature and effect of the contact, it being apparently assumed, once again, that the contact had value in itself.

A case could be made for the opposite belief: we might call this a "bad-seed" assumption that contact with Americans in the Peace Corps encounter is more often than not harmful to the third world. In support of this alternative, we would cite three analogies, none of them farfetched. In our own society, there are many people who believe that the impact of social workers on welfare recipients is psychologically damaging to the latter: the more contact, the more damage. According to some, the effect of urban ghetto schools is to dull the minds of the children who attend them: another damaging contact. In the third world itself, it used to be assumed that peaceful contact between European and colonial peoples was beneficial to the latter. In retrospect, colonial rule did much harm; the literature of the third world is full of testimony to the psychic scars inflicted by Europeans on the people they ruled. (One example, the colonial school, was discussed in Chapter 3.) There are many similarities between the colonial and Peace Corps situations. In both cases, the outsider — European or volunteer — is literate and skilled (and usually of a different skin color), and he comes bearing the message of the "modern" world. Faced with this analogy, the American too frequently replies that Americans are *better* than the European colonialists, a point of view that will not be persuasive to the Europeans, nor necessarily to the people of the third world.

This "bad-seed" interpretation is, of course, no more valid than its "good-seed" opposite. We have presented it in an effort to show two extremes, within which many shadings of opinion may lie, and to reveal the unspoken attitudes that have guided Peace Corps programming. Both helpful and damaging contacts can result from the Peace Corps encounter, and in the great majority of cases, neither we nor anyone else knows what has happened.

The second, or development assistance, concept of Peace Corps programming assumes that what matters most is development — the goods, attitudes, skills, energy and institutions needed to eliminate poverty and misery. Volunteers, it is believed, should be assigned to where they can most effectively aid the course of modernization. Priorities must be established to speed the flow of volunteers into the right jobs. Though this concept is commonly articulated in the Peace Corps today, the change is far from complete. Because of the vast backlog of problems created by the good-seed approach, few people dare use it in defense of their decisions; but nonetheless it lurks behind much of the planning of the agency even yet, introducing an element of irrationality into the end-product of development assistance thinking.

The rational approach of development assistance weighs the relative value of teacher training or secondary school teaching, of public health education or clinical medicine, of credit cooperatives or consumer cooperatives. Yet here, too, illusion tends to creep in. The technology required to do the jobs specified is assumed to be relevant to any culture, and so you insist that the host country assign each volunteer a counterpart who is supposed to soak up the skills of the endowed American and turn himself into a readable copy of the foreign transient. The people themselves are expected to be anxious to receive new skills. The ruling powers of the host countries are wistfully thought to welcome the

social revolution implied by industrial technology.
Development is seen in the third world, by elite and common people alike, as some kind of magic which over-
endowed Westerners carry around with them in their
suitcases. Thus, when a host-government ministry in-
vites a group of volunteers, and when a village eventually
receives those volunteers, the general expectation is
that their very presence will set in motion heaven-sent
forces of "development" which will begin to resolve all
the problems of poverty without sweat or effort on the
part of either volunteer or host. This general belief in
development as sleight-of-hand, which readily instigates
Western fads among exotic tribesmen, places any foreign
technician or Peace Corps volunteer in the position of
magician. Development assistance normally has enough
problems without being encumbered by magical thinking on the part of the sending nation too; yet, creeping
through the back door of the Peace Corps, the good-
seed concept often makes its entry by insisting that the
maximum number of volunteers produces the most
effective Peace Corps. Many overseas programs, operating under an impressive cloak of rationality in their
development assistance efforts, have become vastly over-
blown Byzantine complexes of undecipherable projects,
each claiming exclusively the "right" gospel and unique
access to some facet of the host country, all in competition with each other but by no means all making a
solid contribution.

Immediately we are thrown back to a concern that
occupied the first part of this book: intervention in the
affairs of others. Given the third-world environment,
given the physical and psychological surroundings in
which change is taking place willy-nilly, the readiness of

Americans to intervene in any part of people's lives stems from an overwhelming feeling that any change would be for the better, and that Americans' technological wealth proves their competence to direct change. On the other hand, a growing awareness of, and respect for, the relationships people have worked out over the centuries with their environment and with each other — and an awareness of his own ignorance — will lead the foreigner not to interfere at all. This is not a semantic dilemma; it is the dilemma of the confrontation between two cultures. It seems to us that successful Peace Corps volunteers have found a way of working with their fellow man despite that dilemma. They have, by going overseas, accepted the fact that they *are* intervening in other people's lives. But most of them, in our experience, take a more modest view of that intervention than do their fellow Americans — even Peace Corps officials back in Washington. The most successful volunteers have found for themselves a role as "agents of change." Such agents, according to our interpretation of the Peace Corps experience, usually work along these lines:

To adapt and apply improved productive technology. Volunteers often become painfully aware that much of what they have to offer, both in technology and in the capsule of attitudes surrounding it, is not relevant to the society in which they are working. After seeing how often Western technology has failed in the third world, they see the reasoning that caused an Indian official to issue this warning to agents of change:

How many of you have been told or heard that the cultivator is slow, lazy, unwilling to accept new ideas, or unwilling to make any changes? Most of you have. I should like to stress that the farmer in every country, whether it be Etawah District of India, an out-of-the-way village in the United States, France, Mexico or elsewhere, is conservative. He is conservative because he is smart. It is a fortunate thing that the farmers are conservative. If they did not demand proof, if they did not want to see results, if they were not careful in exchanging something that they know will work for something they know nothing about, then the world would have many more famines than it has experienced to date. . . . Is it reasonable to expect the farmer to risk his year's work and the food for his family on the advice of a man who cannot prove by nature's own method the techniques he is trying to get the farmer to accept?

To understand the local culture. Volunteers, coming to understand what the Indian official was talking about, learn to respect the foreign culture which surrounds them; they then become wary about committing aggression on their hosts' way of life. Peter Easton, a volunteer in Niger, wrote:

In many respects, one has to admire a people who, in these rude physical circumstances, has been able to develop such an expansive, colorful and human model of life. . . . It is no wonder that these people have difficulty understanding foreigners who seem so preoccupied with development goals and significant projects that all grace goes out of their manner of life and out of the images they hold up to the new society. Mausa people are not fundamentally opposed to change. They have in fact modified their farming methods considerably over the last 100 years. They will welcome any innovation which clearly promises to expand their scope of life. But they do not see the point in disrupting the traditional rhythm and style of their days in order to introduce graceless changes, which add nothing to, and may detract from, their human stature. Working graceful changes, however, is a slow, daily task.

Volunteers who, like Easton, see their task as helping their hosts to work "graceful changes" are liable to see themselves, not as bearers of the technological and cultural gospel, but as apprentices and learners who, at best, will only make a small difference in the way the third world changes. Often it is they themselves who change most. They come to see the meaning of the words of the West Indian poet Aimé Césaire, apostle of Negritude:

> Hurray for those who never invented anything
> for those who never explored anything
> for those who never conquered anything
> hurray for joy
> hurray for love
> hurray for the pain of incarnate tears.

To explain the intruding world culture. Whether we like it or not, man is not a noble savage living in balance with immutable nature. The world is intruding on each of us with greater insistence every day. This intrusion requires each of us to change. An expanding world-view is essential to rapid and successful adaptation to modern conditions. Thus the agent of change not only can decide for himself how he must change to meet the new conditions; he also can explain to people of an isolated, traditional society the nature of the world beyond their horizon. More important, he can display, in himself, free choice in matters of cultural adaptation — thus making it possible for "modernization" (that machine which appears to roll over man like an invincible juggernaut) to be a matter of individual perception and selection.

It should be apparent that as an introducer of the great world into the mud hut, the Peace Corps volunteer — even the best one — can be replaced at a fraction of the cost by a transistor radio, which has the added advantage that you can turn it off. It should also be apparent that a Peace Corps volunteer plus a few transistor radios — the disembodied voice of change plus the flesh-and-blood apostle — will tend to reinforce each other. One hopeful product which might emerge would be an understanding that diversity in adaptation (keeping in mind the remarkable resistance to symbols of "modernity" of, say, the gypsies) is possible and probably desirable.

To increase the options of the aided. Whether one's picture of the third world is that of Aimé Césaire, or that of Hobbes, who saw its life as "nasty, poor, solitary, brutish and short," we can identify certain crucial differences between the Peace Corps volunteer and his hosts. The material differences are crushingly obvious, but, in part because the volunteer bears no capital goods in his hands, this is not our primary concern here.

The difference in options — in life choices — is as great as the difference in per capita incomes. That young American who is the volunteer is rich in choices: in careers, in styles of living, in marriage partners. (He even had service in the Peace Corps as an option.) But the person of the third world is as poor in options as he is in material goods: in most cases, there is only one form of work (at times *none*) open to him; he is bound tightly into a culture that regulates his way of life in great detail; even his marriage may be arranged. He has, that is, very few choices as to how he will live, or sometimes whether he will live; and what is true of the individual is true also of communities and even societies in the third world: their options are extremely limited. Closely related to this poverty in options is the third world's poverty in communications. Villagers, and even urban slum dwellers, live in isolation from sources of information and ideas: few messages reach them from outside their restricted world. Fewer still travel from them to their government. By contrast, the American is deluged with far more information and ideas than he can possibly absorb; he can feed back information, too, by voting or by telling some pollster which TV show he likes best. The American's wealth in options is due in large measure to his wealth in communications. He has access to a wide range of ideas about how to live his life and also to the information necessary to put those ideas in practice; the man of the third world has neither.

The task of multiplying human options frequently is served when the volunteer acts to open new channels of communication for the people of his community. These channels may be between a village and the outside world, or among groups within the community; communication with the volunteer, though essential to his task, has no lasting importance in itself, since it ends with his departure. The goal of increasing communication is, as the cases presented in this chapter suggest, perhaps the most constant element in volunteers' experiences. Indeed, one of the truest measures of a volunteer's success might be whether new channels of communications were opened that outlasted his presence — a measure based on different assumptions from the counting of contacts between volunteers and their hosts.

Peter Easton's efforts at "graceful change" involved creating new lines of communication in a small African town. During his service, Easton was involved in the planning and building of a community center and the beginning of an African-language newspaper. Both were "firsts" for that community. Raising the money for the center, which was entirely locally financed, required the bringing together of people of different classes who had never had much communication. If the center lasts — and the way it was planned and financed indicated that its chances were good — it will be the focal point of a new kind of communication in that town. So, of course, will the newspaper.

To increase the power of his hosts while deliberately limiting his own. Power is perhaps the most important issue in the encounter between the volunteer and his hosts. If the volunteer is to help his hosts gain a greater mastery of their environment and therefore over their own lives, his work must increase their power, and by the same token decrease his power, and that of other outsiders, to direct the future of that community. If the people have become more independent through his action, they are less dependent on the volunteer. His co-workers must feel a sense of property about the projects in which they are engaged — that they, rather than the volunteer, "own" the ideas — if those projects are to outlast the volunteer's presence. His task is to help the people gain sufficient power so that his presence is superfluous: that seems to be what is meant by the Peace Corps expression "working yourself out of a job." Of course, this task is not completed during one volunteer's two-year stay, nor probably will it be within a century; but it is the ultimate goal of the agent of change. If he views himself as the agent who creates channels by which new information and ideas flow to and from his community — without seeking to censor the content of those new communications — the volunteer steers away from the dangerous role of cultural imperialist. He does not attempt to limit the people's options to those preferred by himself or his culture. He will act as what Peter Easton called "a true support and stimulant to his [local] colleagues in this task of carefully creating out of all modern possibilities the forms most apt to deepen and broaden their people's style of life."

It must not be assumed that the agent of change, working toward the goals we have extrapolated from the Peace Corps experience, will be free of the political dilemmas of development assistance. For instance, he may be unhappy when, after having successfully increased people's options and stimulating their power to handle their own affairs, they should choose to live in a collectivist fashion. They might even choose (or submit to) a Communist government. The vast majority of Americans would not like that. Yet it is our experience that most Peace Corps volunteers would support the right — the need — for the people they have been working with to make those decisions themselves, and to live with the consequences, even if it were to be proven some day that the U.S. State Department actually did know best. A more likely outcome, given the history of the last two decades of decolonization, is that people will actually continue to choose, or submit to, strongly authoritarian, militarist governments. The consequences of such a choice — or submission — must likewise be endured by those involved, if the lessons of the Peace Corps job are to be followed to their logical conclusion.

There are other dilemmas of development assistance in which money, materials and priorities run head-on into the irrationality of human need. Poverty-stricken people will frequently choose, as their first attempt at self-help, a project which merely adds decoration to the insufferably meager life they are forced to live — such as beautifying their town square or painting the religious center. The agent of change who is unable to understand the people with whom he is living will feel much internal anguish at such moments, especially when he himself can envision a project which might begin to break the cycle of poverty.

The agent-of-change role makes heavy demands on the Peace Corps volunteer. It may be that some personality types cannot accept this role. If a person believes in his bones in authority, if he believes in a single set of cultural values, if he cannot accept the idea that giving power to others excludes him from the decisions as to the use of that power, then he is poorly suited to the role. At best the role is a tough one; if its implications are repugnant, it becomes impossible. People who aspire to the conventional forms of leadership — who want to "own" the results of their action — seem to have made poor prospects, since the agent of change has to support the leadership of others. The volunteer's job is a discipline centered on other people, not a popularity contest centered on himself. Those who get pleasure out of watching others gain power and leadership are well suited to the job.

After studying the experience and opinions of fifty volunteers, W. J. Burns, deputy director of the Peace Corps in India, concluded that successful agents of change are people "who can refrain from imposing their own values on co-workers and supervisors, who involve them in joint problem-solving, who help them relax in their presence, who accept themselves, who are willing to compromise, who let the co-worker and supervisor know that they are approved and accepted, who reward rather than punish, who seek to build self-confidence in the other person, and most of all, develop trust, by being somebody they [supervisors and co-workers] can trust."

To win the trust of others, the agent of change must necessarily extend his own trust to them. This implies what is perhaps the most fundamental requirement of the agent of change: he must be willing and able to engage himself at a deep emotional level with people of another culture. If his involvement is real, he has to have a capacity for suffering, for the experience is bound to be painful at times. Pamela Benson, who was a volunteer in India, put it most simply. "You've got to be able to bleed," she said.

Little is known about how to find people who can play this role. Considering its great difficulties, one of the surprising conclusions of the Peace Corps experience is that many young Americans have proved themselves able to become agents of change.

chapter 9

AMERICA'S UNSENTIMENTAL EDUCATION

"Ask not what your country can do for you . . ."

In hovels and air-conditioned bungalows, in barn-yards, schools, government ministries and slum community centers — wherever Peace Corps volunteers live and work — we have listened to them groping for words to explain why they joined. Sometimes they quote the famous Kennedy invocation. Behind their search for words one often senses a desperate need to find a cause in which to invest their efforts without fearing that it will turn out to be false.

At a time when the United States was becoming victimized by its lack of realism about the world abroad, a way opened up to change the orientation of significant numbers of young Americans toward the rapidly shrinking world in which they and their offspring would have to get along. Through the Peace Corps, thousands of volunteers stepped up eyeball to eyeball with the reality

of life in the third world. If the experience was unsettling, if the clash of cultures was painful for the volunteer, he had only himself to blame: he had volunteered
and could resign without prejudice at any time. No
career plans were at stake. No commander ordered him
into battle at the point of a gun. He had decided to
make a two-year commitment all by himself. As it often
turned out, this option to decide, this freedom, was a
heavy burden. "I suggest that you decide with care,"
wrote a volunteer to a batch of new recruits — a volunteer who did not want to hang on for his full two years.
"It's a bitter experience to resign overseas, take it from
me." To the new recruits he described how he had joined.
An acquaintance of his had once ". . . said something
about the Peace Corps — he said the Peace Corps is a
game, the most interesting national pastime we Americans have invented since baseball. I think this was not a
very wise thing to say because a game is something you
do for fun without ever having to ask why. . . . Very
soon, I think, the game goes out of it. Then you must
know what you're there for, what you are going to do,
and why."

Other Americans overseas have not had to face their
role in quite such an honest way. For their motivation,
they have been able to fall back on the threat of a court-
martial, or upon a variety of games (Tourist, Recorder of
Exotic Customs, Searcher for Unspoiled Paradises);
or they are mixed up in the foreign aid game ("Help-
erino," as Douglas Nolte calls it); or they are players of
the oldest game of them all, diplomacy. Whatever the
rationale that took those Americans abroad, they have
usually been able to bring enough of their American

baggage with them to barricade themselves effectively from the local culture. They learned little because little penetrated their Hiltonesque isolation. Most volunteers manage to avoid the Hilton syndrome, usually out of preference; where preference is lacking, however, they still are saddled with the Peace Corps mud-hut image, and the unglamorous subsistence allowance paid them by the agency. Living out where the action is, volunteers are bound to learn more than do most other Americans overseas.

Learning on the part of Americans, the third purpose of the Peace Corps as specified by Congress, has proved much more important than the agency's other two purposes of providing skilled manpower to the third world and of informing other countries about the United States. When a volunteer was asked what he expected to leave behind when he departed from a village where he had struggled with organizing cooperatives for two years, he said bleakly: "A long trail of dust — that's what I'll leave behind." Many volunteers would agree with him, and yet even if they leave little but dust behind, they may take a great deal home with them.

As a contributor to development in the third world, the Peace Corps can make no great claims to accomplishment. As we have seen in preceding chapters, the agency is still groping around for useful roles for its volunteers. Volunteers have filled a lot of jobs, but their utility in those jobs, and often the utility of the jobs themselves, is questionable. The rural development effort in Niger is an extremely rare case of a clearly successful program; most other examples of Peace Corps success are the accomplishment of individual volunteers who made it pretty much on their own. These are only a tiny minority of the thirty thousand cases in the Peace Corps. Education, the area in which most volunteers have worked, is the haziest to try to assess. Volunteers have taught in many schools and they have gotten through their two years — but are those schools assets or liabilities to their societies? And did the volunteers who sought to make changes in the schools offer any real improvement, or just Americanization? Such questions today have no sure answers. There is also the possibility, though agency officials don't like to think, much less talk about it, that the Peace Corps may at times have done harm. When foreigners come charging into a society with their cultural or technological gospel, they can lead people down the blind alleys of irrelevance and, more serious, they may undermine people's belief in their capacity to solve their problems. This is what we earlier called the "bad-seed" interpretation of foreign intervention, and it should be said that the Peace Corps has undoubtedly been less guilty of it than are most people intervening in the third world.

Yet an enormous potential clearly exists in the Peace Corps. The agent-of-change role we described in Chapter 8 is a far more subtle and promising approach to intervention than anything that preceded it in U.S. official thinking. This concept does not guide the Peace Corps today, in part because it is difficult to practice by harried officials trying to place thousands of volunteers overseas every year. But the idea has taken root and will perhaps grow, changing its form as the volunteers learn more about the mysteries of development. If the Peace Corps can build on the isolated cases of success that its volunteers have registered, then its help to the third world could be much greater than it has been to date.

The second goal of the Peace Corps is simply propaganda, and few people take it very seriously. Publicists in the Peace Corps and the United States Information Agency can and do trot out testimonials from inhabitants of the third world to the effect that, yes, the Peace Corps has given us a new image of Americans, we have seen that what they (i.e., the Communists) say about you isn't true, and so on, often with accompanying photographs of volunteers and locals grinning at each other. For the volunteers themselves, "I'm making friends for America" is the last refuge of someone who can find no other justification for his presence overseas; you do not hear that line from the ones who see value in their work. All this is self-delusion. Most of the testimonials from the third world are a natural response to the obvious desire of those powerful Americans to hear just that. (In the Philippines, this response is an aspect of maintaining what is known as SIR — smooth interpersonal relations.) No doubt some people in the third world have seen something new in America in the person of some volunteers. Not that this new look is always flattering. Indian officials confronted with the flood of unskilled volunteers that arrived in 1966, may well have revised their view of America as a nation of technicians. But individual impressions, even many favorable ones, do not add up to anything much. Making friends is not making foreign policy. Leaders of the third world would have to be remarkably stupid or naïve to let their opinion of America be shaped by the tiny Peace Corps rather than by the much more powerful manifestations of the U.S. Government overseas: the military, the State Department, the CIA and AID. People in the third world can spot a token as well as anyone else — and indeed a token of goodwill is what many Americans in those other agencies also believe the Peace Corps to be. One Peace Corps official overseas spoke of his feeling that "the military types and the embassy people look at the Peace Corps as merely another trick to keep the natives from getting restless." There is no reason to think the "natives" cannot see through such a "trick."

Yet, though they have not yet contributed much to development and their making of friends is beside any real point, the volunteers have justified John F. Kennedy's idea many times over by what they have learned. What they do with that learning in later years will be the measure of what the American people are getting for their money. In our opinion, we Americans are likely to draw high dividends from our investment in the Peace Corps. Americans are getting a very special kind of education at a bargain price: this is the clearest result of the Peace Corps experiment.

In the simplest sense, returning volunteers have helped to take a lot of the mystery and fear out of the American view of the third world. In 1961, for example, it was an act of daring for a young American girl to take off for what her relatives still thought of as Darkest Africa. Since then, thousands of such girls have proven that it is possible to live for two years in Africa without being eaten by cannibals, raped by natives, or even crowned as a White Goddess. The evidence of their effect can be seen in the common complaint of early volunteers that the Peace Corps is filling up with "bland volunteers." What this means is that the agency is attracting more conventional people, and the trend is due to those early volunteers who showed that you did not have to be a hero or a missionary or a nut to venture into the wilds of the third world.

But the lessons of the Peace Corps experience go far deeper. The founders of the agency expected that the volunteers would come back with some useful familiarity with the third world. They did not anticipate that many volunteers would undergo an intense personal experience that would profoundly alter their opinions of their own society as well as the third world, nor that they would become skeptical of the standard American view of its role in that world. The Peace Corps experience has turned out to be a journey of self-discovery as much as discovery of others. The personal encounter with other civilizations has been painful and unsettling as well as enlightening. Once the volunteer had worked his way into another culture, he was able, in the mirror of that culture, to see his own society reflected. He found that he did not look to others as he saw himself, and he found that the "America" they saw was not the "America" he knew. Not that this happened to all volunteers. Some volunteers learned nothing overseas, others came back with conclusions diametrically opposed to ours. Nonetheless we believe a significant shift in opinion has taken place, and that it has been in the directions we describe here. Where this re-examination of one's premises can lead was well stated by eight volunteers in Ecuador: "The more deeply we examine ourselves the more clearly we realize we are part of a culture whose pride in itself contains, as a corollary, contempt for others. . . . semi-literate in its [Ecuador's] language, nearly ignorant of its culture, we still presume to teach Ecuadorians methods of thought and work that we have inherited from our North American past."

Many explorers of the relationship between the rich nations and the poor turn, at one time or another, to the analogy of Prospero and Caliban in Shakespeare's *The Tempest*. Almost always, the focus is on what Caliban, the third world slob, has to learn from Prospero, the Wizard of the West. Seldom is it suggested that Prospero has anything to learn, except perhaps better ways of converting poor Caliban (as, for example, the "new purpose" in Peace Corps teaching, described in Chapter 3). Prospero already knows it all, and he has the Gross National Product and the guns to prove it. Through the Peace Corps, however, many young Americans have come to believe that Prospero has a lot to learn, about himself as well as about Caliban, if the two of them are to share this earth in peace. Volunteers like those in Ecuador are less sure than they were before they went overseas that they, the Prosperos, have anything to offer; and they are not too sure what Caliban wants or needs. If anything, it may be along the lines of the "agent of change" described in Chapter 8; but they are not too sure even of that.

Volunteers are likely, therefore, to be skeptical of the uses of American economic and military power in the third world. Neither buying people nor bombing them appeals to most volunteers. Not many returned volunteers were impressed when Dean Rusk told one thousand of them in 1965 that "after World War II . . . this unimaginable power of the United States was committed to the decent purposes of the American people." Rusk went on to claim that Lord Acton's dictum that power corrupts did not apply to the United States. "Power has not corrupted the American people," he said. But many ex-volunteers would hold that power has indeed corrupted, not the American people, but the government that actually wields the power. While they are overseas, volunteers typically take a dim view of the older government agencies. "What's wrong with the State Department" is high on the agenda of volunteer griping sessions. In part this is youthful resentment of an older, stuffier bureaucracy; and their low living standards give volunteers a charter to mock those who live on Embassy Row. But there is more to it than that. Volunteers often believe that, because State and AID employees do live in air-conditioned isolation, they never get to feel the texture of the countries which they are supposed to understand. The difference is as much one of style as it is over specific foreign policies. A notable example, mentioned earlier, is the clasped hands symbol that AID insists on slapping on most of its material goods overseas. Whoever conceived that symbol doubtless wanted to identify the contents as an American gift so that the "natives" would be properly grateful. But to every volunteer we have heard on the subject, the clasped hands are offensive and, in fact, more likely to produce resentment than gratitude. They believe that shoving things down people's throats makes them gag.

If Prospero looks different to a volunteer overseas, so does Caliban. Volunteers who have seen the awful gap between rulers and ruled in the third world become as

skeptical of those ruling elites as they are about the uses
of American power. Many volunteers doubt whether
those now in power have the strength and self-confidence to lead their people to the Promised Land. Yet —
and again because of their own personal encounter with
the elite as human beings — volunteers are less likely to
indulge in the sweeping condemnation of those flying
visitors who see only the imitation and the corruption,
the pitiful palaces and pretenses of the new rulers of
the third world. There is a sadness almost beyond description about those elites, torn on the rack between
two civilizations, and the volunteers have seen it. Volunteers who became a part of that environment are less
likely to think of "elites" as a class, but rather of Ahmed
or José with whom I shared my food, a job, happiness
and disappointment; their criticisms will then be tempered by understanding.

Beyond these general attitudes, a lot of volunteers
bring home a new style which they developed overseas.
Any volunteer who did not simply vegetate for two years
had a chance to experience that involvement which, as
ex-volunteer Peggy Anderson pointed out in the passage
quoted in Chapter 1, is a motive for joining the Peace
Corps. Patrick Hare, a volunteer in Honduras, put it this
way:

"In trying to build institutions, the volunteer learns
to respect them and the social processes that keep them
greased and running. I may not respect the policies some
institutions come up with, but at least I now think of
American institutions as something we have to overhaul,
rather than as perpetual motion machines that I should
throw stones at."

Hare hopes that the volunteers will use their new-found organizational skills to reform the Peace Corps itself. Then he relates the volunteers to the problems of their own American society:

"The larger question, however, is not just whether Peace Corps volunteers can learn to swim in the bureaucratic waters of their own organization, but whether a whole generation of liberals and radicals can stop being afraid of the water and teach themselves to swim."

The Peace Corps experience, we believe, has changed many volunteers from people who throw stones into people who know how to swim. Many come home with a determination to overcome the injustices of their own society. They are more likely to make effective agents of change at home than are their fellows who did not go abroad (notably the typical American "radical," whose talent for irrelevance assures the existing order that it has nothing to fear from him). The potential of the former volunteers was brought home to us by attending two political meetings, one of which was conducted by former volunteers. The two groups were concerned with the same cause, and they were made up of much the same sort of people: middle-class American college graduates between twenty-five and thirty-five. The chief difference was that one group was graduate students and young professors, the other was the former volunteers. Despite their similar backgrounds, the contrast in style between the two groups was extraordinary. The returned volunteers were pragmatic and efficient; with a minimum of wasted time, they were organizing themselves to accomplish their purpose. The young academics seemed painfully immature; they acted like teenyboppers compared to the volunteers. They were playing *at* politics, and they seemed more interested in showing themselves off than in accomplishing any particular goal. If they were playing games, it was perhaps because they had never had the opportunity to play anything but games. But the volunteers overseas had been forced to confront power, to seek their goals in dealings with people whose values were often opposed to their own. Toughened by the often painful experience of grappling with those who hold power in the third world, aware that change is slow and moves half a step at a time, they did not waste their time — as the other group did — bemoaning the fact that the world contains a lot of people who are hard to like. Their idealism was tempered with a pragmatic sense of the possible, and, at the same time, they had developed a taste for involvement; such people can be formidable.

Of course, not all returnees will become agents of change at home. A good number undoubtedly will follow the gray-flannel route and become indistinguishable from other contented members of the middle class. A few may withdraw from a society in which they do not feel at home. But those who do seek to participate in social change will, we believe, be good at the job.

At present, the former volunteers are to be found in the largest numbers in government, teaching and in graduate schools. Peace Corps alumni are now spread all over the governmental landscape—not through any organized patronage for returned volunteers, but through a heightened interest in public affairs that seems to be a product of the experience. A total of 12 percent of all former volunteers are employed by the federal government, many of course by the Peace Corps itself. Since nearly 40 percent of returned volunteers are currently back in school, this leaves a large chunk of the gainfully employed remainder in the government.

Primary and secondary education have benefited from the Peace Corps. One-third of the employed ex-volunteers are teaching. In August, 1967, New Jersey Commissioner of Education Carl Marburger said he wanted to find teachers who had what he called "the Peace Corps syndrome" to live and teach in the inner-city schools so as to establish there something of the same contact that exists in the suburbs between local community and school. At about the same time the *Philadelphia Sunday Bulletin* reported that the schools of that city were going to employ more than two hundred former Peace Corpsmen when the new term began. The heavy Peace Corps influx resulted from a campaign to recruit the returning volunteers before they left their countries of assignment. The same kind of zeal to hire former volunteers was shown several years before in the Cardozo tract schools of Washington, D.C., the vast Negro slum region of that city. The result there was greater vigor and a sense of hope in the schools — and a predictable increase in conflict between the new wave and the old guard. In all these cases, it is likely that American schools have gotten an infusion of teachers who have learned about the importance of cultural factors in education — something that is perhaps easier to see overseas than in one's own society.

Former volunteers working overseas for other agencies may ultimately be of more value to the third world than they were during their Peace Corps Service.

The State Department has accepted 57 former volunteers, as of this writing; the U.S. Information Agency has accepted 22, and the Agency for International Development has taken on a total of 209 former volunteers. Most of these are now working overseas. These newcomers to the traditional overseas establishment of the U.S. Government are working at a low level, without significant policy-making authority. But, when they are no longer so junior, they may still remember what it was like living as a volunteer in a peasant community, speaking the local people's language with their particular twist to it, sharing what little they had in their pot; and what they learned as volunteers may add a new tone to their actions as policy makers. At the very least, they should provide a better brand of Prosperos. "Maybe you can humanize the American Empire," one skeptic told some returnees.

In an age of specialization the Peace Corps has rehabilitated the generalist. Volunteer generalists, as seen in cases cited in these pages, frequently acquired a gut-understanding of the development process, and proved themselves competent to search out and coordinate the many resources needed to get a project going. The basic skill in this is communications, and volunteers have shown that they can learn to become effective communicators: not just in learning a language, but in handling all the messages relating to the deadly serious business of survival in a dangerous world. The ideal generalist, as the Peace Corps has come to look on him, is one who is not totally unskilled but who has some understanding of a lot of things. In contrast to the specialist or technician, he has not committed all his energies and attention to one way of solving problems. Typical of the generalist is Ralph Bolton, whose experiment in agrarian reform was described in Chapter 6 — a man with a smattering of academic subjects and a large amount of curiosity to find out what works. By 1967, some younger Peace Corps officials like Stuart Awbrey, then editor of the *Volunteer*, the agency house organ, were beginning to talk in McLuhanesque terms, telling themselves that the Peace Corps had to learn a radically new style if it was to function in a predominantly nonliterate world. The solution to development problems, in their eyes, lay less with one-shot gimmicks (chemical farming methods, better business procedures) and more with finding a *role* for themselves (and, by extension, the United States) in that great sea of struggling humanity we have called the third world.

The Peace Corps has also had the effect of stimulating other movements that make use of low-skill generalist manpower. By its example, and by its assiduous cultivation of its own image, the Peace Corps has inspired a remarkable number of imitators. As of 1967, close to fifty Peace Corps-style programs had been started in other countries, plus, of course, VISTA, the U.S. domestic Peace Corps. Some of these were imitations by other developed nations; even De Gaulle's France started the "Volontaires du Progrès." But some voluntary programs were taking root in third world nations: Tanzania, Ethiopia and Panama are examples. Their potential importance is great. People are the great bottleneck of development; it is obvious that the nations of the third world cannot afford highly skilled technicians to act as the intermediaries between those trapped in poverty

and the means to escape their condition. Low-paid or
voluntary service by youth with high motivation would
help break this bottleneck. If the Peace Corps has stimu-
lated thinking along these lines, this could turn out to
be the agency's greatest contribution to the manpower
needs of the third world.

The Peace Corps itself, after seven years, is still the
young swinger among the federal agencies. The Shriver
spirit of creative anarchy survives. In no other governmental bureaucracy, and in few businesses, is there such
freedom from the encrusted weight of tradition. One
example is the habit of self-criticism. This was institu-
tionalized in the Peace Corps through a Division of Evaluation, headed from the early days to 1968 by Charles
Peters. Contrary to the usual procedure, which makes
of internal inspection an efficient whitewash machine,
the Peace Corps not only listened to what evaluators
reported was going wrong overseas but often acted on
their observations.* Peters, often supported by Shriver
and later Vaughn, beat off efforts to gut evaluation of its
critical content. Internal questioning goes on throughout
the agency. Under editor Awbrey, the *Volunteer* maga-
zine, once a medium of self-congratulation, became a
battlefield where broadsides could be fired against Peace
Corps policies. Generalists and amateurs on the government scene continued to be given priority in staff
hiring. Discrimination, either by race or sex or age, has
seldom marred the Peace Corps. Young women, for ex-

---

* We have made much of the learning ability of the Peace Corps.
The unique evaluation process has been partly responsible. For a
description, see Meridan Bennett, "Evaluation and the Question of
Change," *Annals of the American Academy of Political and Social
Science*, May, 1966.

ample, have been able to rise far more rapidly in the Peace Corps than in other bureaucracies. It has been a different kind of government agency, one which values learning, innovation and self-awareness over clerical efficiency. One example among many is that in 1967 Vaughn himself put in some time as the "training officer" for a Peace Corps training program. In terms of status, the State Department equivalent would be for Dean Rusk to go work for a while as a junior officer in an embassy overseas. The opportunity to learn in such a situation is enormous.

Of course, there is a penalty to free-swinging innovation. "People in a hurry," says the mordant philosopher, Eric Hoffer, "can neither grow nor decay; they are preserved in a state of perpetual puerility." In 1967, the Peace Corps was still hurrying and still, in many cases, paying the predictable price of haste. It was still failing to meet its own impossible promises, as in India, where it talked about making a "dramatic and meaningful contribution" to the solution of India's basic food problem, and contributed a horde of volunteers without skills or useful assignments. Nor had the agency yet found an adequate programming process. Martin Kaplan, an official of the World Health Organization, sums up his experience with various aid programs in the third world in these words: "The techniques for acquiring aid are quite well known. They are the formulation of a project by foreign consultants (sometimes unkindly defined as those whose expertise is in inverse proportion to the length of their stay in a country), followed by an official request by the government concerned, the screening of these requests by the donor agency, and the implementation of the surviving projects." The Peace Corps, not immune from these well-established techniques, busily rounded up large requests for volunteers, often misrepresenting their skills. When critics of the "numbers game," as expansionism is called in the Peace Corps, protested that unskilled generalists were being deluged on supine recipients without proper regard for the jobs they would be doing overseas, Peace Corps officials trotted out their backlog of requests and said, "They are asking for bread; shall we give them a stone?" In 1967, however, there were signs that the agency itself was starting to de-emphasize sheer numbers.

The Peace Corps, in 1966 and 1967, appeared to be undergoing the rites of passage that would mark the end of its youth. The early dash and glamor were rapidly fading: the agency had lost its status as a novelty. Many people in the Peace Corps were discouraged; the problems of the third world, and indeed some of the agency's internal contradictions, appeared less easy to conquer than they had in an earlier, more optimistic day. More countries were criticizing the Peace Corps and cutting back their requests for volunteers. For the first time, it looked as if the agency might before long come under serious criticism at home as well.

Yet another trend was visible also. The Peace Corps was beginning to digest and apply the many lessons of the volunteers' experience. It was only a beginning, for the time lag from learning to application is necessarily long when the process involves a drastic change in habits. But the signs of change were there. Even the mood of discouragement was evidence that an internal readjustment was taking place. An optimist would have predicted, in 1967, that the Peace Corps was on the verge of a great advance in which the agency would apply what it learned so that the majority of volunteers, not only a fortunate few, would have the profound experience that the Peace Corps at its best can provide.

Ironically, it was at this time that the Peace Corps was being threatened by forces that lay outside the agency's control. Acceptance by Congress and the general public continued high, but in 1967 there was a sudden drop in the heartbeat of the Peace Corps: the rate at which Americans were applying to be volunteers. Intensified recruiting efforts produced few results. Some in the agency attributed the fall in applications to old-fashioned, "square" recruiting tactics, and others felt that competing service programs like VISTA were draining off some of the potential volunteers. In 1967, applications to VISTA rose while those to the Peace Corps fell, perhaps because the nation's inner turmoil caused people to look more to the home front.

Another explanation, however, appeared to be more basic, and more painful for Peace Corps officials to accept. It lay in the growing distaste for the federal government and its foreign policies among the college students who have provided the great majority of Peace Corps applicants. By 1967, students were turning, often violently, against the federal administration, and most did not make much distinction between the Peace Corps and other parts of the Washington establishment. Peace Corps recruiters found the climate on campus increasingly hostile. "That's enemy territory these days!" one official exclaimed after a tour of several universities in late 1967. The era of good feelings between campus and

Washington that began under John F. Kennedy ended during the Presidency of Lyndon B. Johnson, and the Peace Corps was caught in the backlash. The actual differences in policies between Kennedy and Johnson were undoubtedly far less than the difference in their images as seen from the campus. However, as we noted in Chapter 6, people act on their images, and in 1967 the student image of Johnson was hardly one to attract students to federal enterprises. Doubtless, also, the shift in opinion did not apply to all students; but it was probably greatest among that minority who otherwise might have joined the Peace Corps.

The revelation in 1967 of secret CIA subsidies to a series of American enterprises overseas may also have hurt the Peace Corps by discrediting the federal government. Third-world officials, and many students at home, found it hard to believe that the Peace Corps was not giving shelter for U.S. undercover agents abroad. Such a connection, to our knowledge, has never existed. Shriver instituted a ban on any involvement with the CIA, and the Peace Corps has tried to weed out applicants with any intelligence background. We know of no cases in which either staff or volunteers have gotten involved in intelligence, though of course it may have happened — one of the sorriest results of the CIA's undercover deals is that everyone is now suspect, since it is virtually impossible to prove that you are *not* a spy. In a couple of countries, the resident CIA man has approached the Peace Corps representative with a request that he collect political intelligence from the volunteers; but in each case known to us the Peace Corps man has refused the request. One thing is certain: if there are any spooks in the Peace Corps, they are very rare — far rarer, be it noted, than among overseas members of the American academic community.

Both at home and overseas, the increasingly warlike appearance of American policy posed a threat to the Peace Corps. One staff member back home after four years overseas said: "Volunteers are going to their jobs overseas this summer [1967] with an insoluble set of contradictions surrounding them. U.S. foreign relations are finally catching up with the Peace Corps." The war in Vietnam was the most dramatic of these contradictions. In the summer of 1967 Vietnam caused a crisis within the agency over the right to dissent. Bruce Murray, a volunteer in Chile, wrote letters to both Chilean and United States newspapers stating his opposition to the administration's war policy. Murray was dismissed, and Washington issued an order forbidding volunteers from using the Peace Corps as identification in writing letters to the American press. The ban was rescinded, after volunteers in other parts of the world started firing off letters, in effect daring Washington to dismiss them all. As of this writing volunteers are free to identify themselves with the Peace Corps in writing to American (but not foreign) papers. Vaughn's decision to allow this degree of freedom was typical of the Peace Corps style and was in the tradition defined by Harris Wofford when he called the Peace Corps an "antiestablishment establishment"; it is hard even to imagine that any other federal agency would allow people on its payroll to use its name to attack administration foreign policy.* Doubtless the volunteers' readiness to rebel against censorship

---

* Strangest of all, Bruce Murray himself did recruiting for the Peace Corps after his dismissal. He said the value of the Peace Corps experience should not be overshadowed by what happened to him.

helped shape Vaughn's decision for, as Awbrey later wrote in the *Volunteer*: "The current generation has taught the Peace Corps that it has less to fear from political issues than from restraints on their discussion." Not all volunteers are particularly concerned about Vietnam. Among those who are vocal, however, the great majority are opposed to the war. Volunteer hawks have been sighted, but they are as rare as bald eagles.

On the war in Vietnam, and on the underlying issue of the uses of American power overseas, the Peace Corps, as a federal agency, found itself caught on a middle ground that was rapidly washing away under its feet. There was less and less room for the Peace Corps in the widening gap between those, typified by President Johnson, who believed in free-wheeling use of American power to guide the destinies of other nations, and the dissenting minority that opposed the administration's policies of intervention. On one side were those who equated the Peace Corps with the CIA; on the other side were those, like *New York Daily News* columnist Ted Lewis, who complained that the CIA was *not* infiltrating the Peace Corps. In the growing division of the American people, Peace Corps officials could not and did not oppose the policies of the administration that employed them. But volunteers and ex-volunteers were under no compulsion to be silent. Since they are still mostly under thirty, and since the conflict over America's role abroad tends to parallel the conflict of generations, it is not surprising that most ex-volunteers — at least most of those who speak up — are found among the dissenters. The man who, more than anyone else, has stated the viewpoint shared by dissenting volunteers and ex-volunteers is Senator J. W. Fulbright. In his remarkable speech before the Honolulu Bar Association in 1967, Senator Fulbright spoke of the "false and dangerous dream of an imperial destiny" for the United States. Fullbright saw the hope of avoiding that interventionist destiny — the degeneration into standard Great Power politics of the American Dream — as lying in the hands of:

. . . *this generation of young men and women who reject the inhumanity of war in a poor and distant land, who reject the poverty and sham in their own country, who are telling their elders what their elders ought to have known — that the price of empire is America's soul and that the price is too high.*

Appropriately enough, Fulbright mentioned Peace Corps volunteers as dissenters no less than three times in his speech.

The volunteers, speaking with the brash insistence of youth, are struggling to redefine America at home as well as abroad. In their redefinition of national purpose the young dissenters seem to want a new, participating kind of social order. They want to shed dependence upon paternalism, which they view as a kind of narcotic that deadens the individual's sense of responsibility to society. They see the dangers not only of the elitism of the right but of the liberals as well; they are often suspicious of the paternalism of, say, the Democratic party and the intellectuals. The young dissenters are few in number; they face a huge array of forces against them in the cacophony of present-day demands for revision of

American society. They face the opposition of those who want to preserve the status quo, which, whether labeled as liberal or conservative, in the United States often comes close to being the foundation for the most massively powerful imperial system in the history of civilization.

So, ultimately, we have returned to a theme touched on at the beginning of this book. Seen in the broader setting of the society that gave it birth, the Peace Corps is only one of the faces that America presents to the world. Today that face is eclipsed — unfortunately, in our opinion — by the mask of power. Yet the subtle and modest outlook that has emerged from the Peace Corps experience is as legitimate an expression of the American character as the currently predominant belief in the nation's manifest destiny. The volunteer who speaks of "working graceful changes" is as much in the American tradition — no more, but no less — as the general who lusts for a chance to bomb China. The president who appoints himself the savior of Asia is as much in the American tradition — no more, but no less — as the volunteer who wrote that "the villagers had to speak to me first before I was able to speak of anything meaningful to them." To Americans considering their role in the world, to third-world leaders considering — among many other questions — the possible meaning of the Peace Corps to their societies, it is important to remember that neither of those two faces can claim the exclusive right to express America.

The split image of the two faces of America adds an ironic twist to the succinct comment on Peace Corps potential made in 1964 by Charles F. Gallagher of the

American Universities Field Staff. After observing Peace Corps operations in Tunisia and Morocco, Gallagher wrote:

It seems clear that what the Peace Corps is contributing cannot be the principal ingredient, or even an important ingredient perhaps, for forming the new society being shaped in North Africa . . . but it can be one of the subtle spices which will help give that society a fuller flavor.

Most volunteers would be gratified to know that their efforts had resulted in the addition of a subtle spice: it would be reward in full. But, whatever history's final comment on the Peace Corps, we venture to guess that its spice is most likely to be tasted in the volunteers' own society.

index